Photography Tips and Techniques

Author:

Craig A. Pardini, MPR, ACE

Editor:

Kathy Ireland-Pardini

Photographs by: Pardini Photography and Weddings
www.pardiniphotography.com
240.426.0098

This book is comprised from articles and tips that I wrote based on my popular Facebook Photography Tips and Techniques Group. This is geared toward anyone having passion in the art of photography or looking to further your development and knowledge in the art of photography. These tips are developed for beginners, up to professional level photographers. Whether you use a DSLR, Point and Shoot, Nikon, Canon, Pentax, etc., this book is for you!

Learn the techniques that you need to know to capture the best images possible. This book will serve as your how-to guide giving basic and advanced photography tips, camera settings, composition techniques, equipment purchasing suggestions, and much, much more!

This book is dedicated to my amazing wife, Kathy Ireland-Pardini. Thank you for being my partner in life and in photography. Thank you for all the time you have spent taking care of my life and making it better!!!

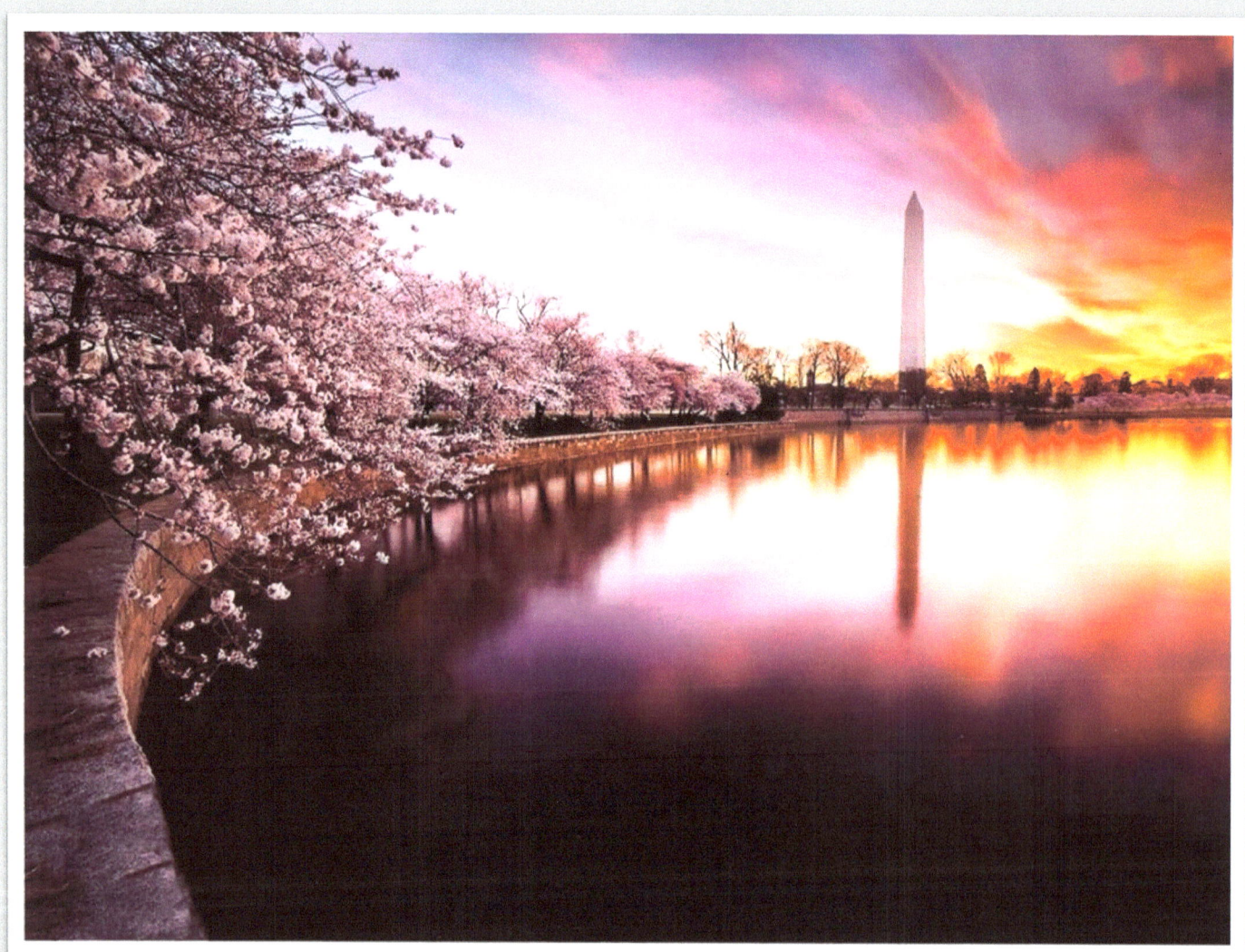

Contents

Taking Better Fall Photographs

Fall is in the air!!!!! Can you believe it???? With the cooling temperatures and the appearance of changing leaves, plus the season of pumpkins everywhere, we are getting excited for our absolute favorite time of year. That's why I'm focusing on capturing the beauty of this colorful season. Here are my best tips for taking great fall photographs:

Try the Panning Technique:

Switch your shutter speed to around 1/8th. Zoom in on a part of the tree, leaf or pumpkin that you want to capture. As you hit the shutter button, move your camera up and down or side to side ever so slowly. Your

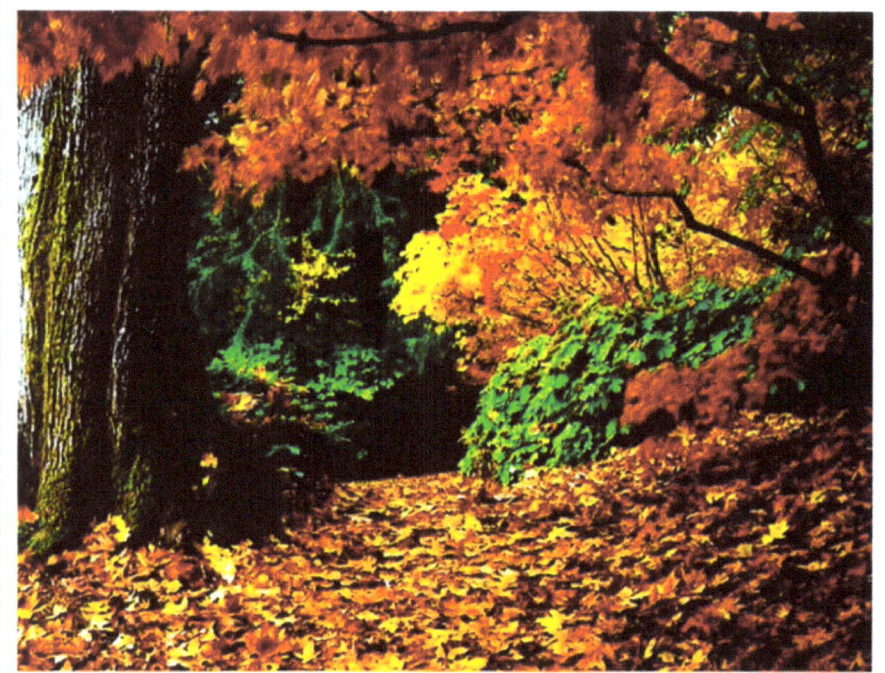

photograph will end up with a nice movement blur causing the leaves to look like they are blowing in the wind. Can't get the hang of the panning technique? Wait for a windy day and use a slow shutter speed to capture the motion.

Use a Polarizing Filter:

A polarizing filter will not only decrease haze that is common at this time of year, it will also help you capture the saturated colors of fall. A polarizing filter can also increase the contrast in your photos. If you don't have a polarizing filter or are using a point and shoot, you can still reduce haze. The air is the clearest in the morning and after a rainfall. These are really good times to shoot, especially landscape shots which could be washed out by any haze.

Set Your White Balance:

You want to make sure to turn off auto white balance when shooting fall colors. There are a few white balance modes that will help you capture warm pictures and enhance the fall colors: shade, cloudy and daylight. If you had to place them on a warm scale, shade is warmer than cloudy which is warmer than daylight. If you were to shoot in 'cloudy' on a sunny day or shoot in 'shade' on a cloudy day, your images will be warm and will really emphasize the colors of the season. You can also set a custom white balance.

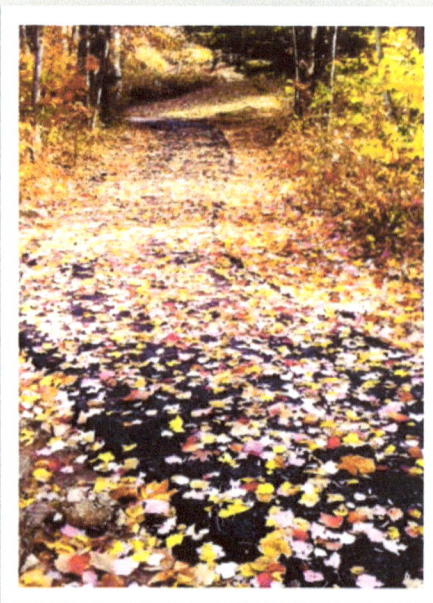

Underexpose Your Photos:

Because the colors are so vibrant during fall, you want to make sure you capture them accurately. By underexposing a few stops, you will deepen the saturation of the colors. You can then use your favorite photo editor, such as Photoshop to enhance your photo even further by playing around with the contrast and vibrance levels.

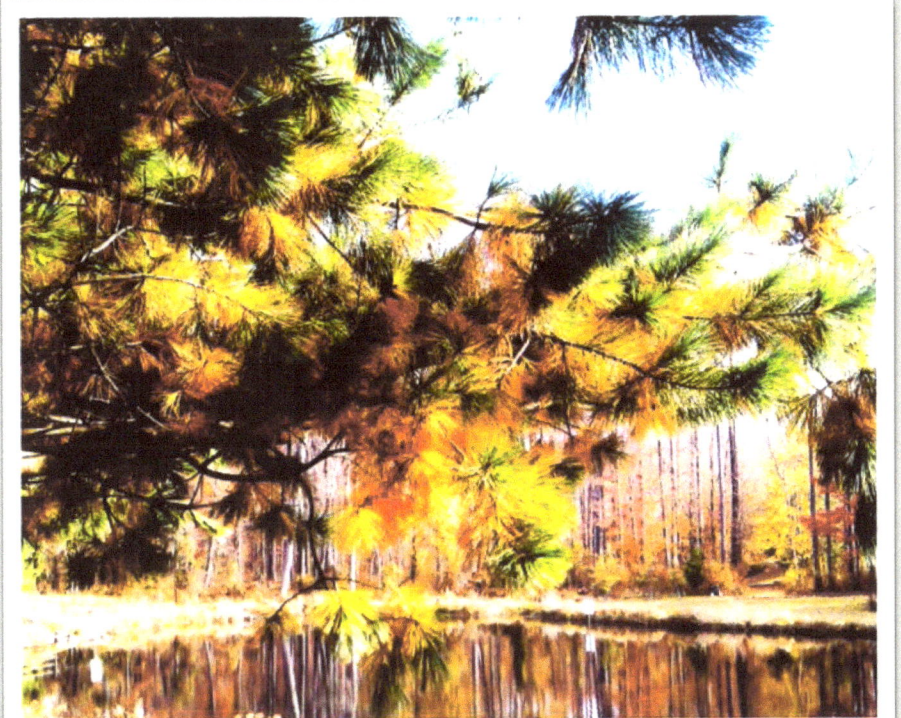

Look for Contrasts:

A great way to show off the great colors of fall, is to look for contrasting colors. Reds pop when they are up against greens. Yellows shine when displayed against a blue background such as the sky.

Shoot Some Macros:

If you do not have a macro lens…Do not worry! Just set your camera to the macro setting, it's usually a 'flower' on your setting dial. Tripods also come in handy to help cut down on camera shake, so you can really focus on the leaves.

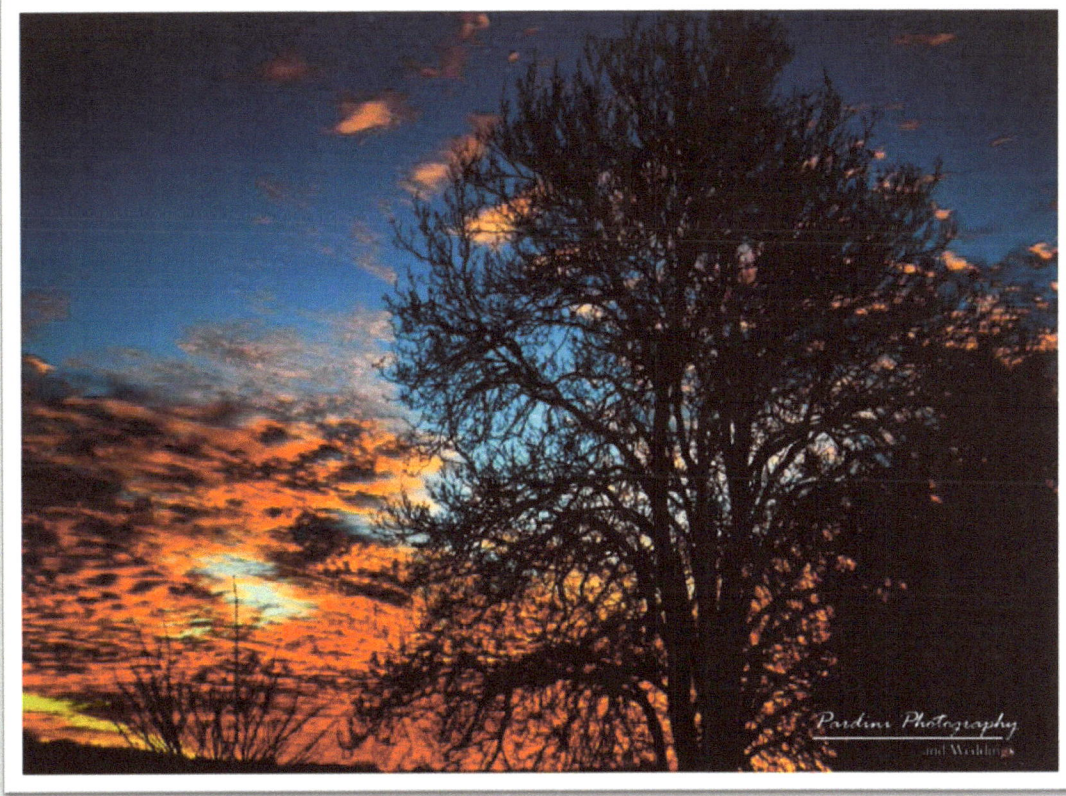

Taking Better Christmas Photographs

Christmas and holiday parties means getting lots of family and friends together and cool decorations. And getting the family together usually means lots and lots of photographs :) Below are a few of my favorite tips to help you take better photos this holiday season. You may use a small point and shoot digital camera or a huge digital SLR. It doesn't matter, because the principals of photography are pretty similar regardless of the equipment you are using... With these few tips, you can improve your family photos, and have the perfect Christmas / holiday photographs that your whole family will die to have a copy of.

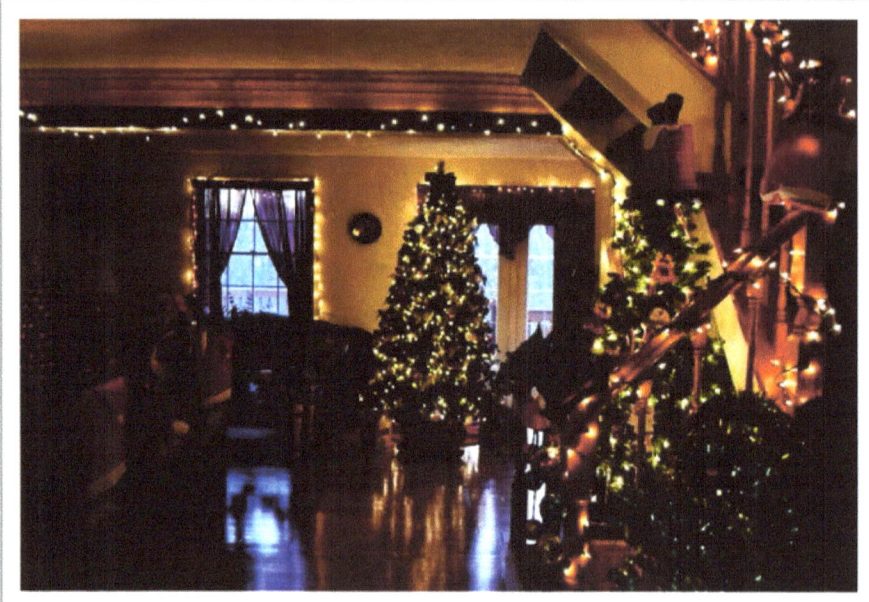

Take a Few Test and Room Shots:

Before people start showing up, take a few shots of the ambient light in the room. If you use manual settings, this is especially useful, because you can figure out the best aperture, ISO, and shutter speed settings for your images before your family comes around. Although light through the windows will probably change after several hours, electric lights will not fluctuate. Given this, you should be able to stay within a range of settings, provided you stay indoors and in similar light settings. This will also give you a good opportunity to take room shots of decorations before anyone gets in your way. I always allow 10-15 minutes prior to anyone's arrival to take decoration and room shots.

Do Not Make Them Pose:

'Say Cheese'! 'Look Happy'! Line up and pose, etc...Posed photographs are unnatural and do not really do a lot, except show your family and friends pretending to smile! Approach family photographs like a photojournalist. There's an important event happening, and you are trying to capture it, as it happens and show a 'true documentation of the event'. Is someone laughing? Is someone opening a gift they always wanted? Did grandpa fall asleep? Did dad sneak outside to smoke and got caught by mom? It can be far richer and more enjoyable when you look back on

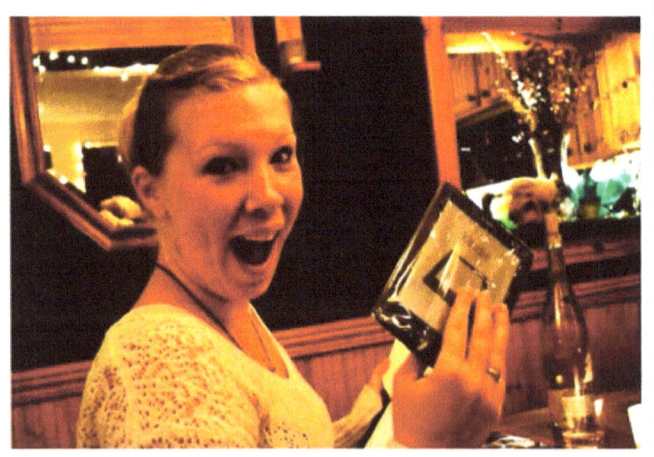

these pictures to see people as they were, doing their own thing. When you pose, you're only capturing the fact that they were there, smiling rigidly…

Think About Light:

The main rule of photography is about capturing light. How is the room you're in lit? Is it dim or dark? Is bright light coming in from the windows? Is there warm light coming from the light bulbs, lamps, or Christmas ornaments? Lighting is probably the single most important part of good pictures and can make or break them. Pay attention to the colors present in the room and use different settings to try and capture them. At the very least, try to keep your subjects from being ruined by backlighting or flashed brightly in front of a black shadow background.

Do Not Be Afraid of the Manual Settings:

Manual ISO, Aperture, and Shutter Speed settings are not complicated if you learn a little bit about the elements of exposure. There's no shame in using automatic settings; they're quite useful in situations where light, people, and environment change rapidly. However, there simply are kinds of pictures that an automatic setting doesn't have the artistic nuance for. Especially if you're trying to capture warm, soft, glowing light from Christmas decorations and low light environments, manual settings are sometimes the only way to go. Some cameras do not have an "M" for Manual setting. These might have a "P" for Program mode. Familiarize yourself with the camera and play around with it, shooting test shots before the big party. Do not be afraid to experiment and mess up a few dozen shots! And if manual continues to be a huge struggle, the auto setting is only a few clicks away.

Take Pictures Multiple Times:

Bracketing is an important word in the Photographer's vocabulary. Since digital photography has made taking a gazillion pictures so cheap, take as many as you can. Remember, that moment will never happen again, so taking the same picture twenty times and picking the best image is better than taking it once and wishing you had a better shot.

Be a Storyteller:

Remember when we talked about not posing your family? The photojournalist metaphor still applies. When you're taking pictures, take them with the end result in mind. A good photo should tell a story, even if it's a little one, and you should think about the story you're telling when you take the shot. What are the people in your pictures doing? Are they chopping vegetables, unwrapping presents, watching TV, or getting blasted on eggnog? People are one of the most powerful subjects to photograph because we immediately can feel empathy for them and relate to what they're doing. Capture facial expressions and events, actions, happiness, tears and laughter. When you tell a story with your pictures, you make it easier to return to that moment again, even if you aren't a skilled photographer.

Pay Attention to Composition:

You might not be an artist, but photography is a visual art form. Again, you have to begin with the end in mind; think visually when you shoot. Read up on the golden mean and the rule of thirds for some insight on how to make your shots look more interesting. Too abstract? Shoot pictures only of the subjects you want in your final shot. Don't stand across the room and get lots of details in the shot that don't help it. When you take pictures of the kids, take a knee and get down on their level, so that all of your shots aren't of the top of their head. And don't always put your subject dead in the center of the shot because it gets boring, particularly when you're showing off your pictures later.

Try It With and Without the Flash:

When you bracket, traditionally, you take the same shot with multiple aperture or shutter speed settings to make sure you expose properly. With digital cameras, you have a good idea immediately if you've exposed your image well or not, so try bracketing your image with and without flashing, especially if you're using the automatic setting.

Use the Lowest Number ISO Setting Possible in Dark Rooms:

The lower the ISO, the less grain you'll get in your low light shots. If you're going to have a lot of these, using an ISO of 200, 400 or 800 is better for graininess than 1600 or higher. You may have to compensate for lower ISO settings by using longer exposures and a tripod, but you'll be able to keep your images from being grainy.

Bonus Tip: If It's Not Perfect, Photoshop It!

I said it earlier…that moment is special… and you'll never be able to go back to it. If your shots aren't exposed perfectly, Photoshop or some other photo editing software can give you the tools to make them better. You might take a great composition of a cute moment, but find that the exposure settings are not perfect, or that the white balance is a little off. While you should hope to expose pictures perfectly every time, the fact is this is not likely, particularly if you're picky about your images.

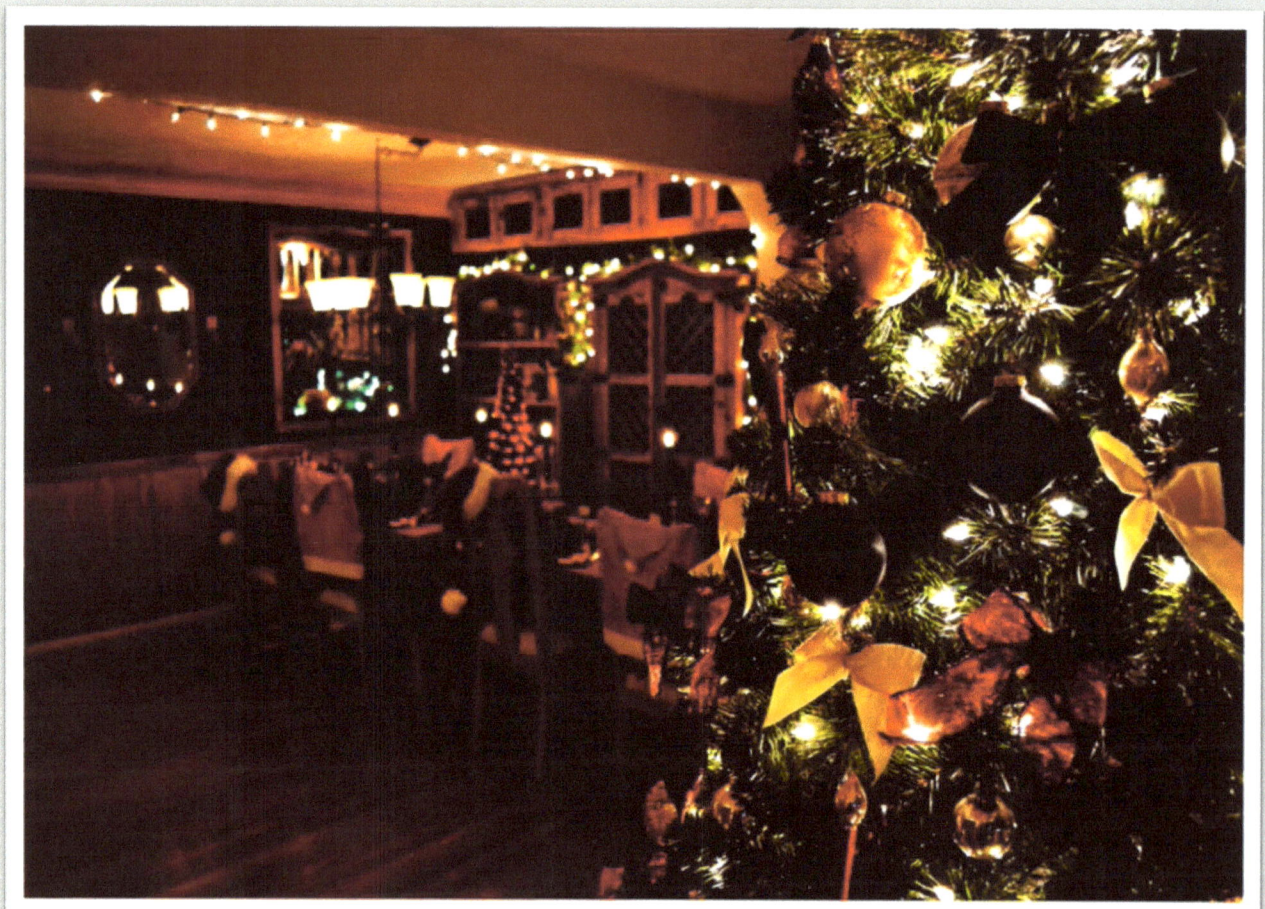

Airshow Photography

This article talks about two of my favorite passions and is a way that I can discuss them both in the same article!

History of Airshows: Man first took to the air in December of 1903 with the Wright brothers in North Carolina. Shortly after that first flight, photographs recording this historical event where dispatched around the world and when aviation photography was born. In 1909, France hosted an event titled 'Le Grande Semaine D'Aviation de la Champagne'. This early air show attracted tons of spectators from around the world to see those daring pilots and their flying machines...

Each year, millions and millions of people all over the world attend air shows. At 'Joint Services Open House' at Andrew's Air Force base in Maryland, almost a million people over two days attends. Of all the millions of people attending air shows, it is estimated that 75% of them in will have a camera!

What to Know Before Going to an Airshow: I suggest that you check the Air Show's rules and regulations for such things as the type of bags that are permitted, etc...

- Many air shows, especially those sponsored by the Department of Defense have strict rules forbidding backpacks of any sort.
- Do not bring food or drinks with you; they will trash it at the security gate... (Just like at the airport :(Some of the money that those vendors pay to be a sponsor can cost several thousand dollars and without their sponsorship, you wouldn't be able to attend the air show for free.
- Bring cash; they do not accept credit cards... Even though most shows are free, most ask for a small donation at the entrance.
- It is a good idea to keep a cooler or snacks at the car. If you don't like paying for food, drinks, or snacks, or don't trust what you are eating, this can be a lifesaver if your stomach starts talking to you...
- Bring sunscreen... And use the sunscreen very liberally across ALL exposed skin. Driving home after the show with severe sunburn on the back of your legs is NOT FUN!
- Sunglasses, hats and earplugs can be a life saver... Even on a cloudy day; runways can still be blindingly bright. If you have any sensitivity to loud noises, the sounds of aircraft engines at close range can be a little loud.

What Sort of Photographic Equipment Should I Bring?

- *DSLR Users*...Keeping in mind that walking around for 8 hours at an air show with 25 pounds of equipment in the hot sun can wear you down.

- *Point and Shoot Users*...Any point and shoot with a reasonable good long zoom will work. However, the weakness of Point and Shoot Cameras is their inability to focus track a moving subject at fast speeds. They are great for shooting images of fast moving jets when they perform a pass maneuver...which is basically a slow speed pass designed to show off the aircraft.

- *Just remember* to bring a lot of memory cards and batteries...

Shooting Tips: This is when good panning and knowing your camera settings comes in handy!

At an air show you will be practicing the art of panning. Panning is defined as: tracking a moving subject at very high speed, and engaging the shutter at the optimum point. In the advanced modes, most DSLRs feature some variation of Auto Focus Continuous, for tracking moving subjects and this is your best friend. You should also set the frame rate of continuous high for the maximum number of frames per second. The most important part is watching your shutter speed. I suggest any speed that is 1/500th second or faster, so the fast moving jets are not a fuzzy little blur! Remember, most jets fly at 500MPH! Your ISO should also be set to the lowest you can shoot with...

At an air show some of the most interesting shots can be of the static aircraft parked on the tarmac. The only problem is the most interesting aircraft usually have tones of people gathered around them. This is a good time to look at interesting details in your compositions such as the wings, tail, landing gear, etc. If you are skilled in Photoshop you can edit the crowed out of the photos giving you the perfect shot!

- You have a great spot on the flight line, and a Blue Angel, F/A-18 Hornet taxis close by with the aviator waving or giving thumbs up. This is an easy shot if you knew it was coming, but not if your attention is elsewhere. Just like wedding photography, you need eyes in the back of your head and a good intuition to capture everything!

- Unless you are fortunate to be in one of the VIP stands, the chances of you getting a show center unobstructed view of the action is slim. So try for the wings of the flight line, where fewer people are gathered.

- Ever seen a Blue Angel F/A-18 Hornet going vertical at 500mph? It is a good idea to use the grid display if your camera has it or if doesn't; use the bottom of your display as a guide. This will help you keep the jet in your range at high speeds and ensure it is in your frame!

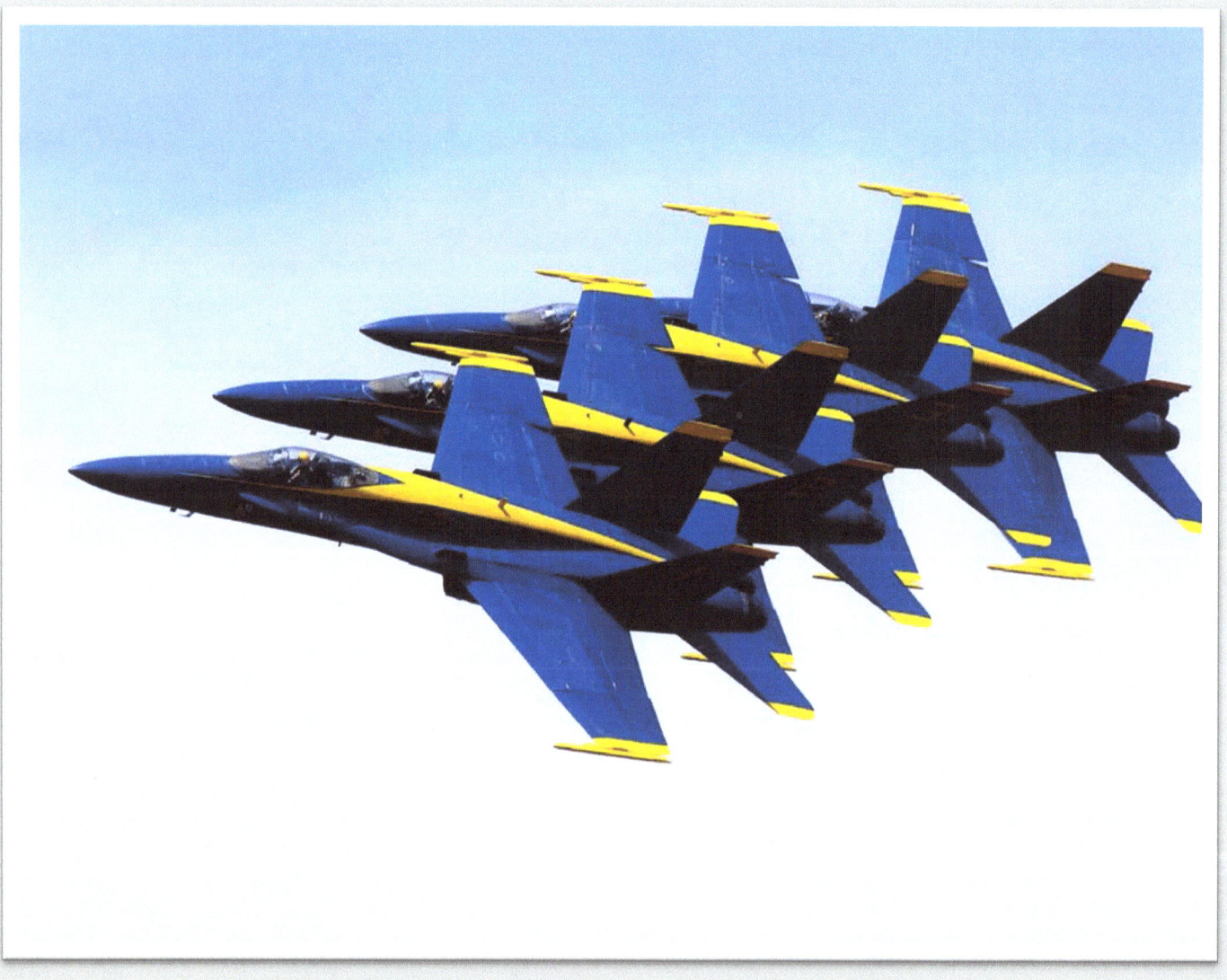

Five Quick Tips for Making Great Black & White Photographs

There are many things that I learned about black & white photography back in the day when we used film: black-and-white film, that is. Some of them translate to digital and some do not… I miss the old darkroom, developer, fixer and hang drying prints :-) I wish that I had room at the house to setup my old school darkroom equipment…

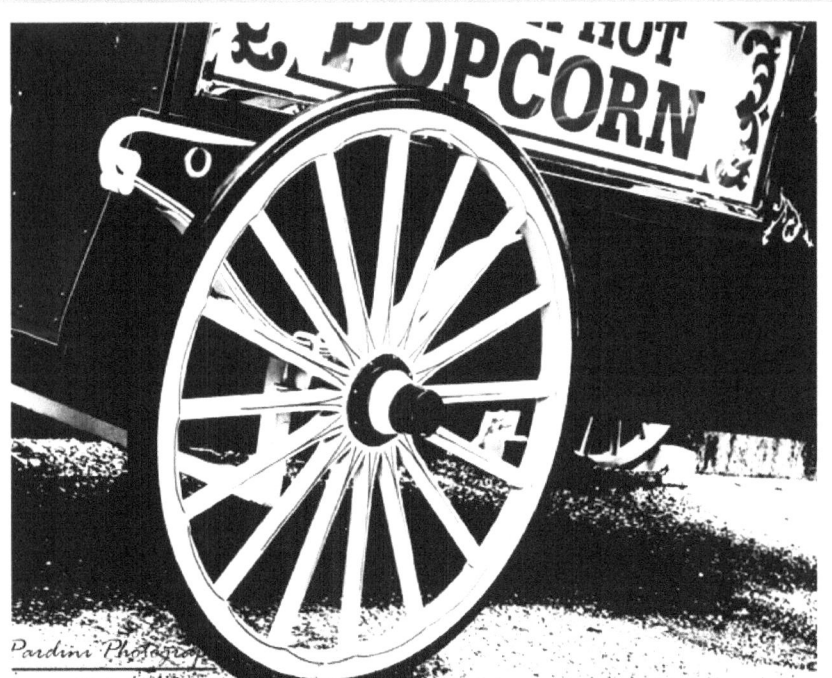

For those of you who want to work in black & white, here are a few tips:

Capture as much data as possible. Shoot RAW in your highest bit depth rate. This is important since so much information can be lost during the conversion. You want to start with as much as you can to begin with.

Do NOT use your camera's black and white mode. This locks you in. Shoot in color and convert for best results.

Shoot with your final result in mind when you're working with your camera. It just makes for better results. Another way to say this is to "think" in black and white.

Think about the actual filters we used to use when we made black and white photos on film and try experimenting with them when you are editing them…

Experiment with some of the great plug-ins that is available for converting to black and white in Photoshop and have fun!

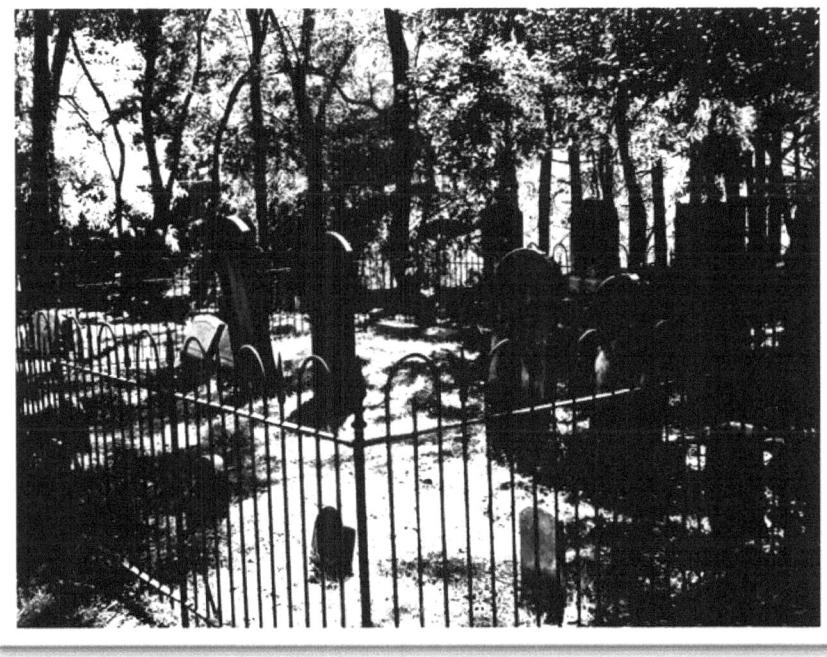

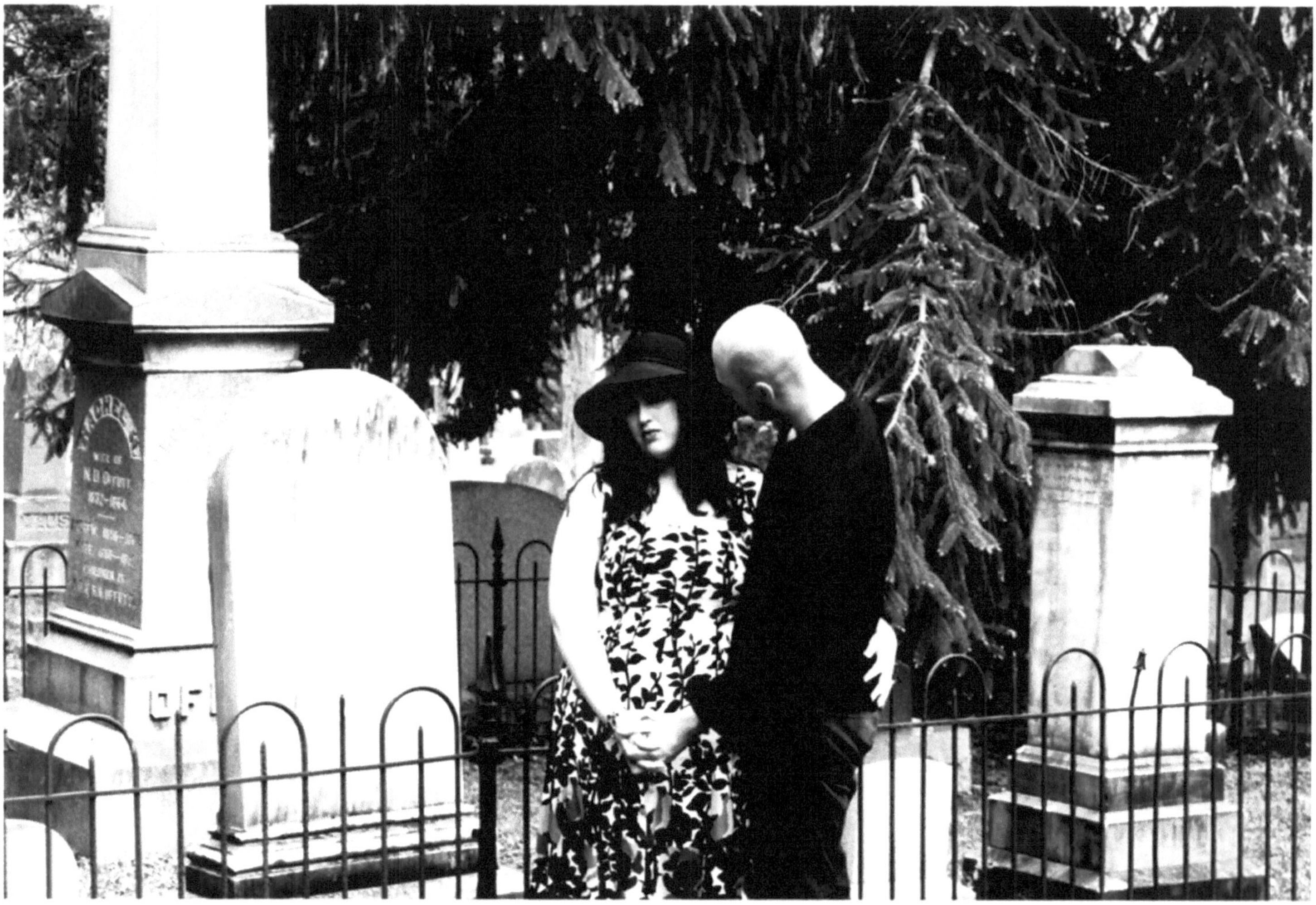

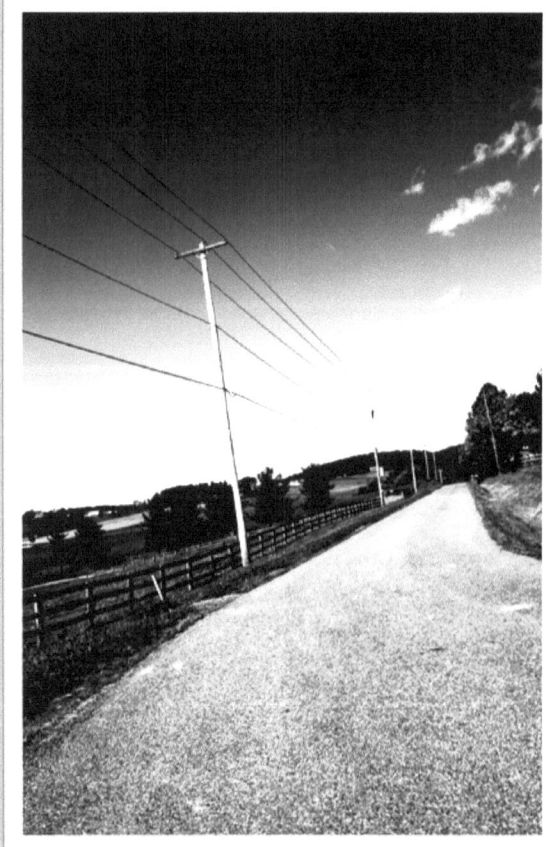
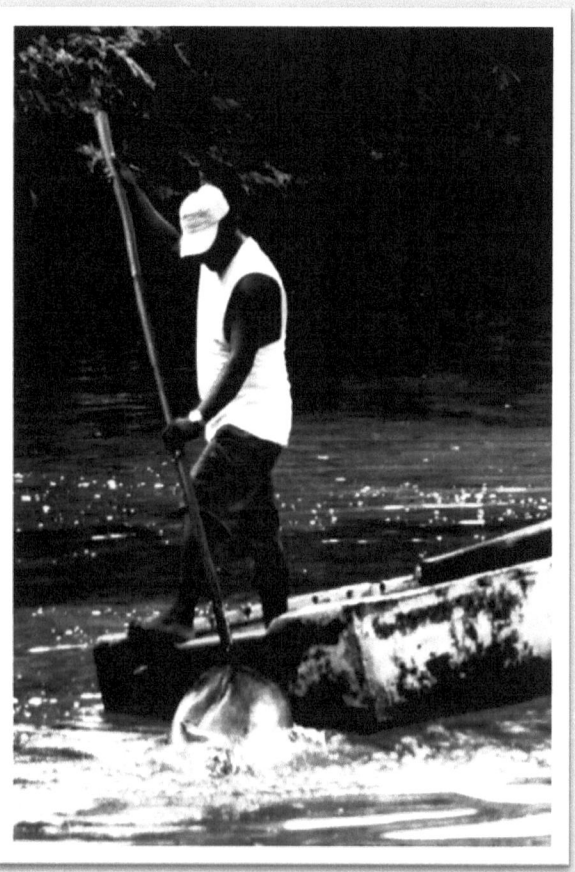

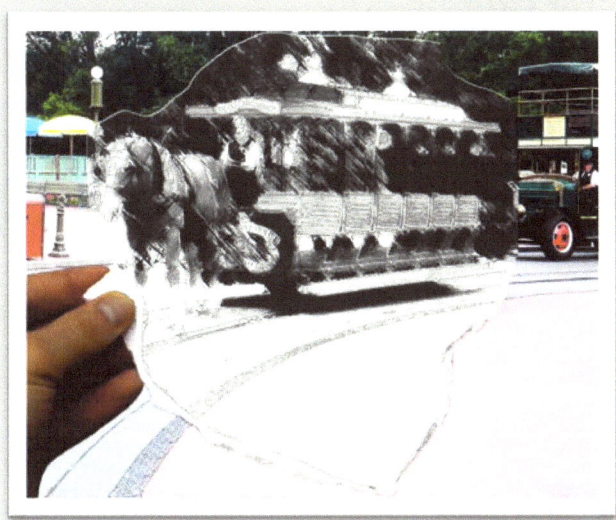

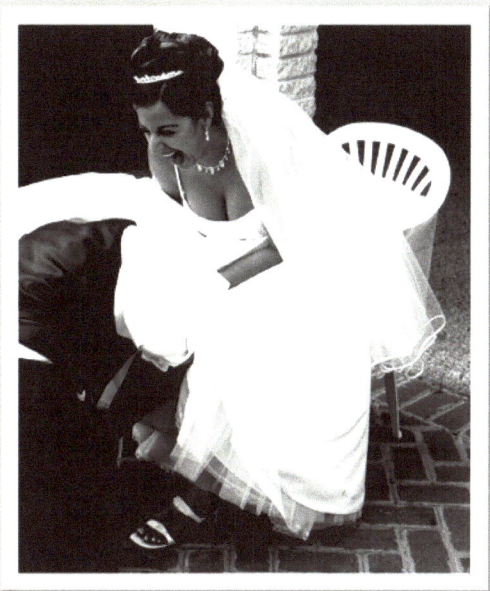

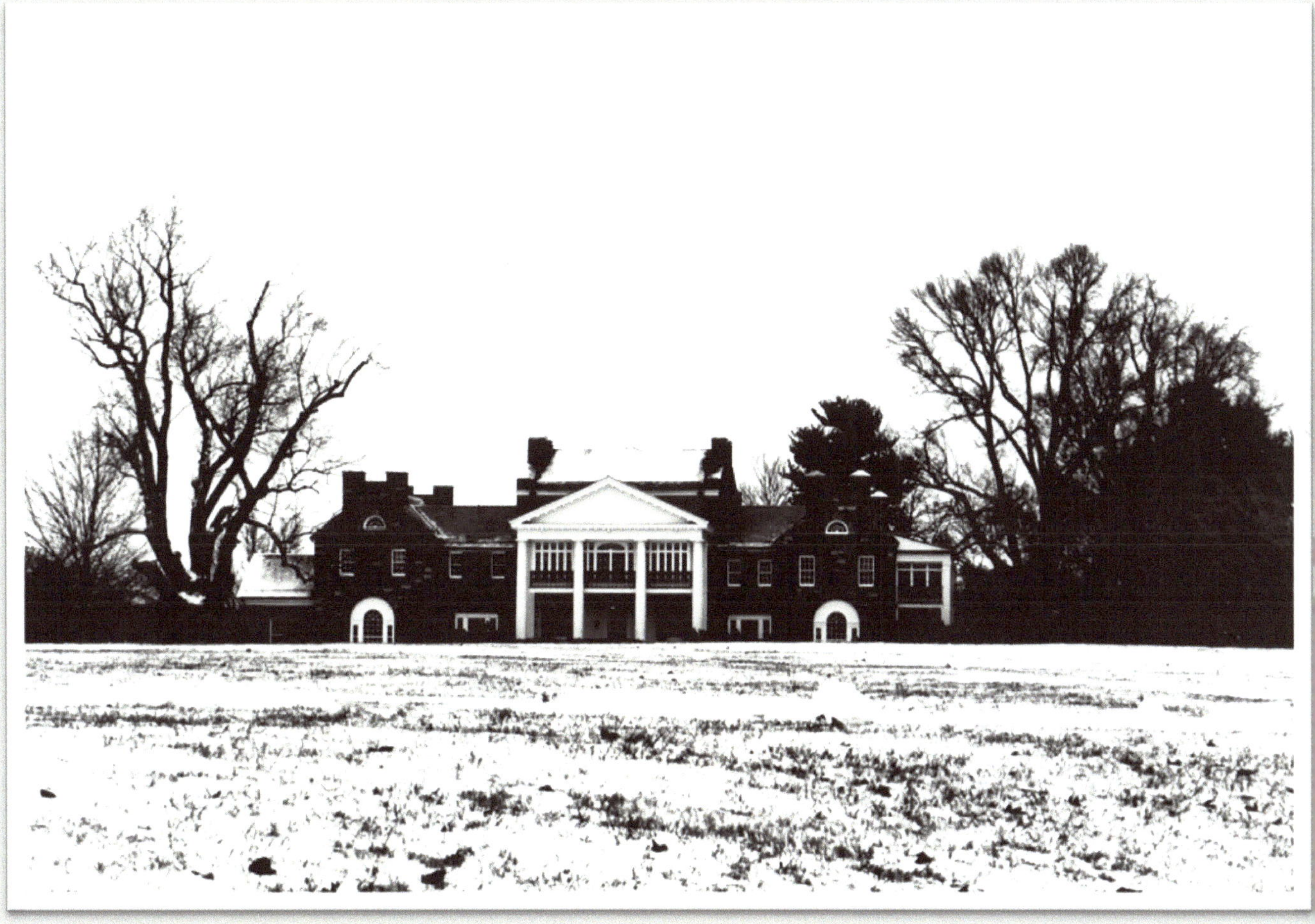

Understanding Composition

You may not realize it, but every time you bring your camera up to your eye, you're making decisions about composition. Easy way to look at it is, composition is how you decide to frame the picture you are taking! There have been many books, videos, articles, etc. talking about composition….just like most, everything, no two people are likely to frame the same shot the same... There are some general guidelines that can help you improve your photos and make them more interesting and engaging.

The Rule of Thirds:

One of the first questions to ask yourself when composing your photograph is: 'What is the subject?' Of all the things,

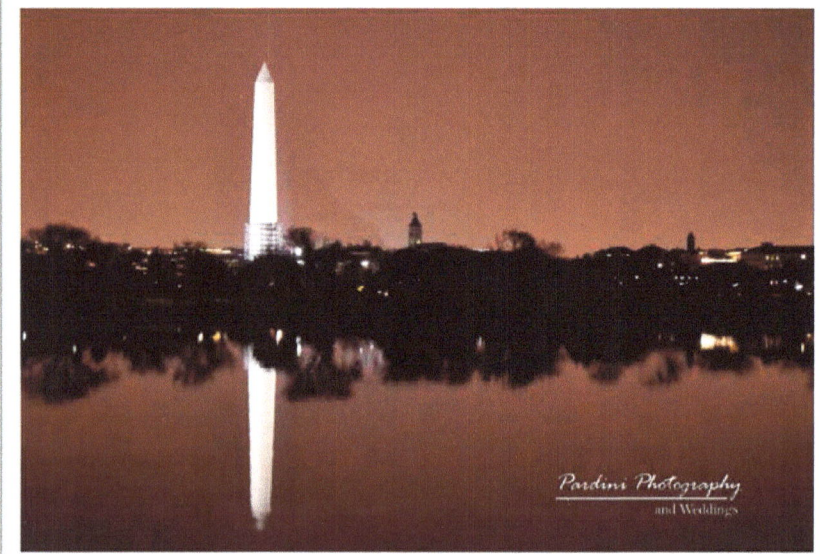

you see in front of you, which one is the reason for taking the photo? Once you've answered that question, you can begin to work on how best to show that subject. The rule of thirds is a guide to help you do just that.

When you look through your viewfinder or at the LCD screen, imagine a tic-tac-toe grid over the scene. Some higher end cameras even have a menu item that allows you to turn on gridlines in the viewfinder. I love this feature! These gridlines are a guide to help you frame your image and won't show up in your final picture. Now, notice where the lines

line up. The rule of thirds suggests that these points are the best places to position your subject. Doing so will generally result in a pleasant and balanced composition.

Try moving your camera so your subject appears where two of the lines meet. The subject doesn't have to be directly on the intersection but somewhere close to it. Try a couple of different compositions to find the one you like best. Shooting digital will allow you to take tons of shots so you have tons to choose from!

These same gridlines can help you to keep your horizons level and the vertical elements in your

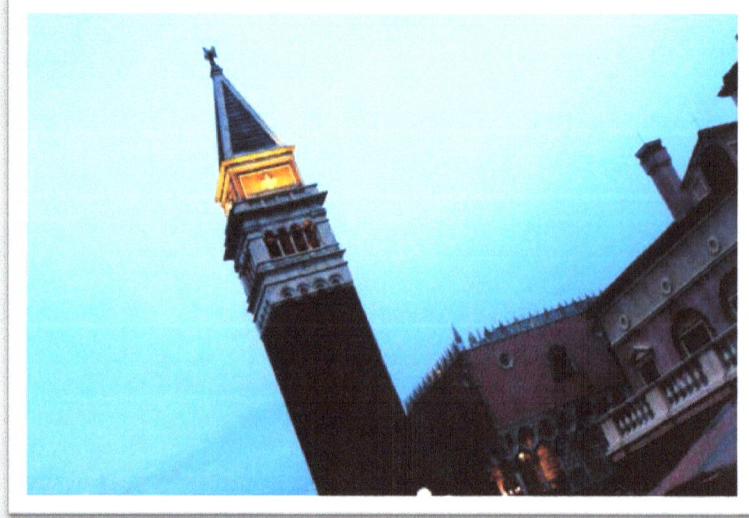

photo straight. Most pictures look better if the horizon is positioned above or below the middle of the frame and not directly in the center of the image. The exception is when shooting a reflection. In this case, having the horizon in the center can work well because it creates equal elements at top and bottom—the scene above and the reflection below.

Watch Your Head:

How many times have you seen this happen? You compose your portrait and click the shutter. Then you look at the image on your LCD screen and, oh no, there's a tree or a light switch, etc. growing out of your subject's head. Always consider the background when composing your image. Look for any distracting elements that might spoil an otherwise nice photo. If there's something behind your subject that you don't want in the final photo you have several options. First, you can change your physical position, or, if, that of your subject. If that's not possible, try changing the focal length.

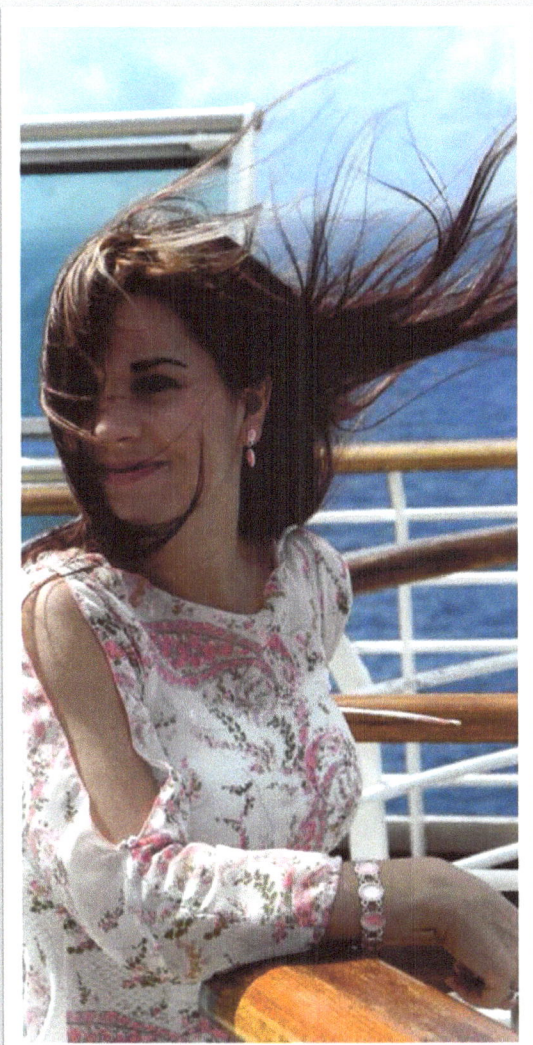

Look Carefully:

Most people aren't thinking about composition when they look at photos, but they do know when a photo is pleasing to look at, even if they don't know why… To improve your composition skills, spend some time looking at the photos taken by people whose work you admire. Pay attention to how they've positioned their subjects within the frame, what their backgrounds look like and what was included in the image and what might have been left out. Now, review some of your own photos and ask yourself how you could have made the picture better by changing the composition.

These guidelines are just a starting point. Remember, for every rule, there is an exception. Don't be afraid to step outside the box if it makes for a better photo.

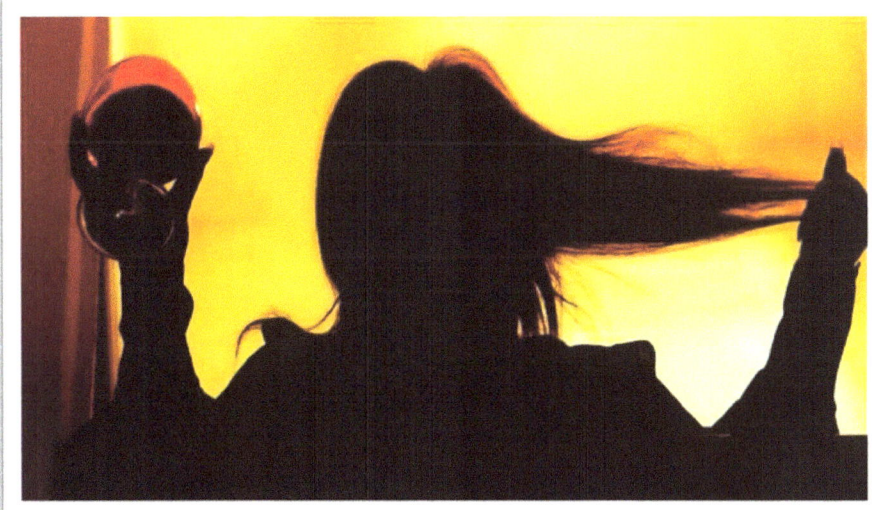

Digital vs. Film Photography

This is a subject that is often asked of me... I don't pretend to offer the 'final word' or 'best answer' but just my

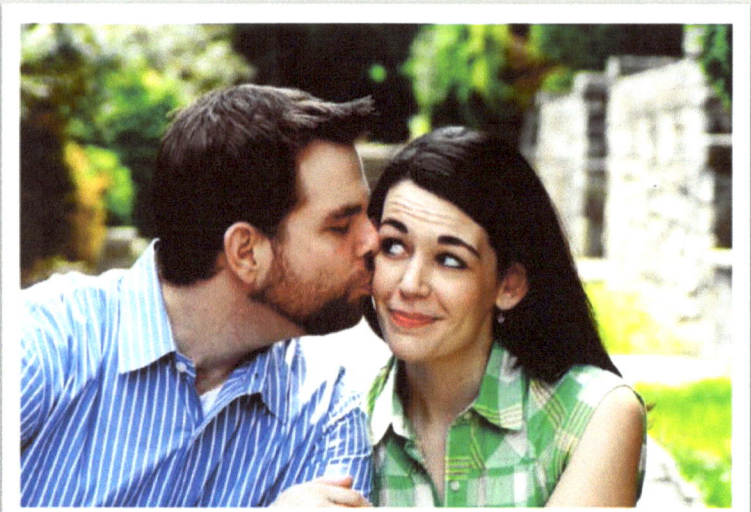

personal perspective. And there's more to this comparison than just a 'pixel count' although that is certainly one issue that needs to be addressed. However, digital photography opens up possibilities that just don't exist in the film world... I will always have a passion for film photography. My first camera was a Pentax K1000, rolling my own B&W film, and processing it in my parent's basement, that I converted to a darkroom! Old school photography is just awesome and especially black and white is crisp and has tons of contrast! If you ever used a darkroom 'burning' technique, you can understand the true fun and skills involved to make it happen! I will try to break this down as much and as fast as I can...

Being a professional wedding and portrait photographer for many years...I was asked a lot back in the day, especially right after digital photography first came in play: 'Why do you use digital photography?' My answer was: I like to refer to digital photography as "digitally mastered photographs." As a skilled Photoshop craftsman, we can alter, darken, lighten, add or take away contrast, enhance, and almost do any changes you may want to your photographs. Some people are skeptical about digital enhanced photography. Just look at it this way, the computer is a digital darkroom and it takes just as much skill as it would in the dark with film, and the finished product looks a lot better. Less than a second after taking an image, our camera will display the image on an LCD screen located on the back of the camera. We can instantly double check lighting, composition and posing! This is one of the biggest advantages to digital we have experienced yet! Keep in mind that most people are using standard digital cameras that are very limited in the functions that are offered and priced

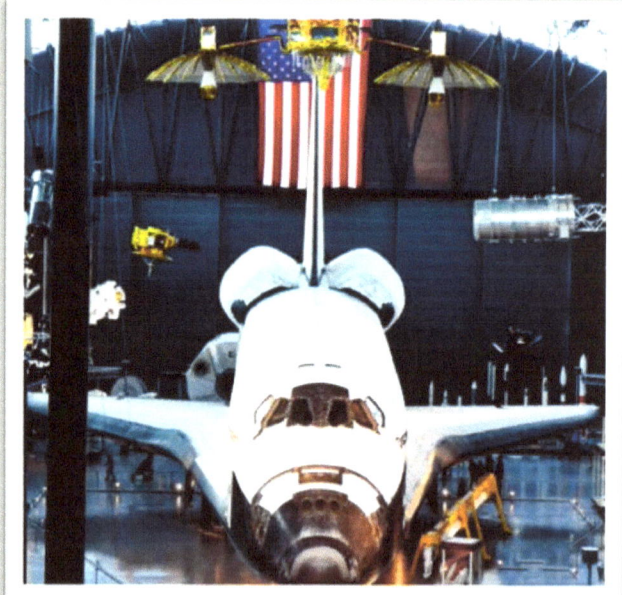

somewhere around the $300 - $1000.00 range. Not all digital cameras are alike. We use several digital, professional SLR cameras that have more functions then a professional film camera and are priced from $6,000+, not including any accessories and lenses. These are some of the advantages of a digital camera:

- The ability to see the image right away. This is our favorite reason for using digital. It gives us a level of comfort because we can see if the lighting, expression, exposure, etc. are correct right away rather than wait to see the film back from the lab in a few days. The ability to change the ISO (or the equivalent of film speed) quickly. This allows us to go in and out of an array of lighting situations without having to suddenly change film to match the light levels from place to place at a wedding.

- A virtually unlimited number of photographs can be captured at an event. This in itself frees us from thinking "we can only shoot 10, 12 or whatever number of rolls of film that is in the client's budget".

- The ability to make black and white and sepia toned photographs from the digital images. When we shoot digital, every photograph can become a black and white and/or sepia image. Parents may want an image in color; the couple may want to have it in black and white.

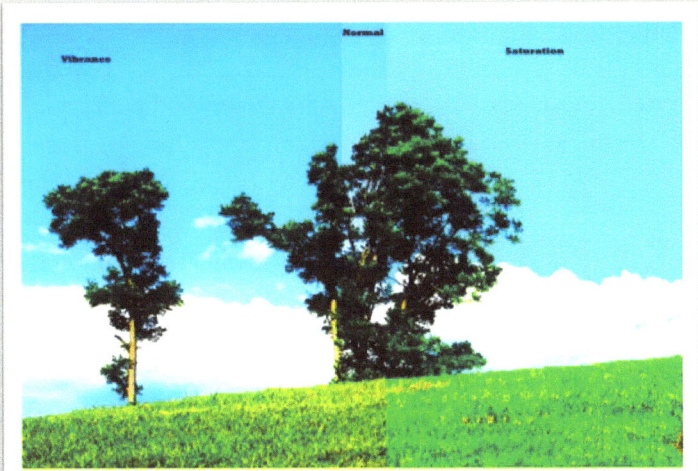

- Freedom to experiment. This is a corollary to reason one. We will often shoot images that we would not even try with film because we will be able to erase it if it doesn't work and modify it because I'll be seeing the results immediately.

So To Give You Some Comparisons:

Film:

As to pixel count, the conclusion I have reached is that 35mm film can potentially contain at least 10 megapixels worth of resolution; how much more will depend on the type of film, quality of the optics used to produce the image, etc. This is equivalent to say a 3900x2600 pixel image file. The advantage of having a high number of pixels is twofold: 1. the more pixels you have, the better quality print, especially at larger sizes, and 2. you have more flexibility in cropping.

But in order to get a digitized file for use on the computer, you must have a very high quality scanner to do this. You must also consider the time element: you take your shots, get them developed at the lab, and once in your hands, run them through your scanner (which at the highest quality can take several minutes or more per image).

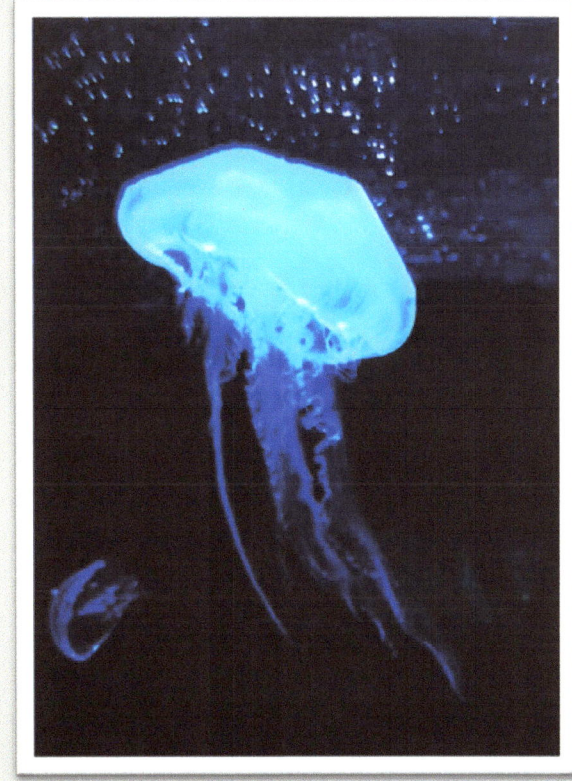

Another important consideration is that you don't know how good your shots are until they're back from the lab. For an experienced photographer, under fairly controlled conditions, this may not be that big a concern, but even there, tricky lighting conditions can be problematic, film can get lost, the lab can mess up, etc. Plus, you're paying for every shot, regardless of whether it is good or not. I can't tell you how much I have spent back in the day on photos that did not turn out or not worth keeping…

And if you are staying purely within the film/chemical area, and not digitizing at all, then you need to own, or have access to, a darkroom. Most shots will need at least a little "touching up" to show all that you're intending for the image. This is potentially a costly, and problematic area, as most can't afford, or don't have ready access to a chemical darkroom.

Digital:

Currently, a lot of cameras have 12 or more megapixels. This is now clearly in the same ballpark as scanned film. So purely on a resolution basis, the best digital SLR's are definitely competitive with scanned 35mm film.

Where digital really shines is in providing immediate feedback, on the scene, when the opportunity is there to adjust and reshoot as needed. You can view the images taken on the camera's LCD Screen, and can assess framing, focus,

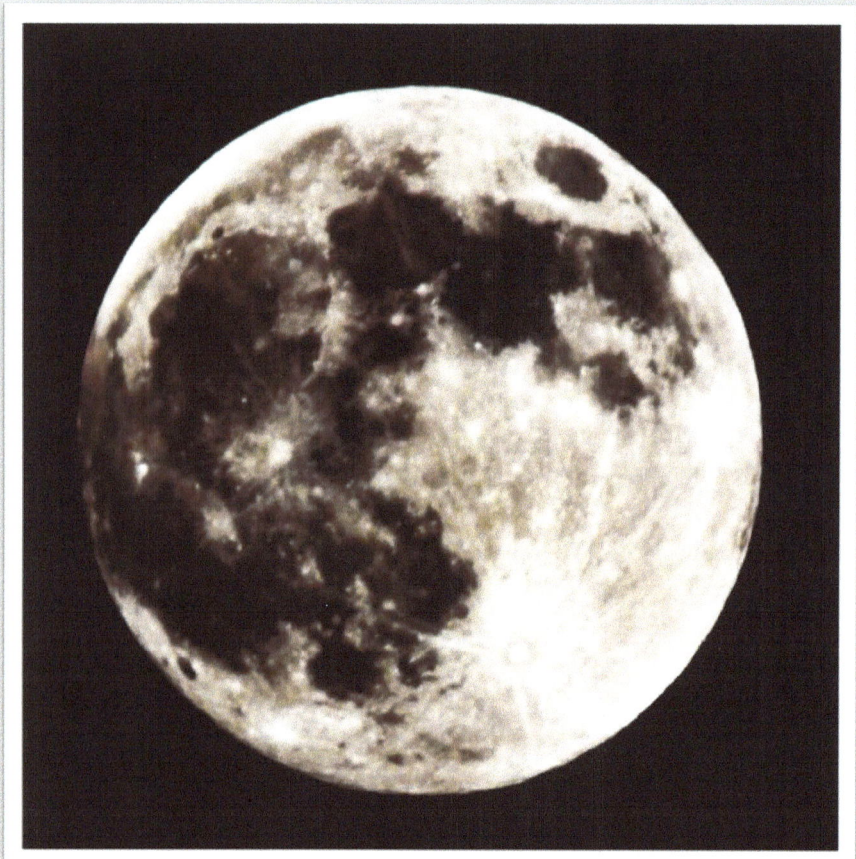

etc. Many of the better digital cameras additionally provide a "histogram" display, which will graphically show whether or not a shot is properly exposed. If the result is not what you're looking for, you can just delete the shot, adjust your camera settings, and keep reshooting until you have what you want. There is no cost per image once you have invested in the equipment, and so one can experiment freely, trying things that you generally would avoid with film.

Another unique advantage in digital photography is ISO, or film speed, control. In film photography, you choose the film speed based on your expected shooting needs. But you run into different conditions, and need a different ISO film, you either need a second camera loaded with this film, or manually replace one roll with another. In digital cameras, all you need to do is change a setting, and you can keep shooting. Some of the better digital cameras offer ISO ranging from 50 to 3200+, which is a very wide range. There is some increase in "noise" (analogous to film "grain"), but even this can be rectified to a fair degree by editing with the right software. And recent technological developments has resulted in dramatic reduction in the noise at higher ISO, and most reviewers conclude that the digital noise at high ISO is markedly better than film grain at similar or lesser ISO.

Whether you get your digital images by scanning or negative film, or from a digital camera, the use of the 'digital darkroom' is extremely helpful. Software is readily available (free or inexpensive at the low end, up to several hundred dollars at the high end), and if one devotes a little time and effort, you can become fairly adept at improving whatever images you start with. And again, experimenting is free.

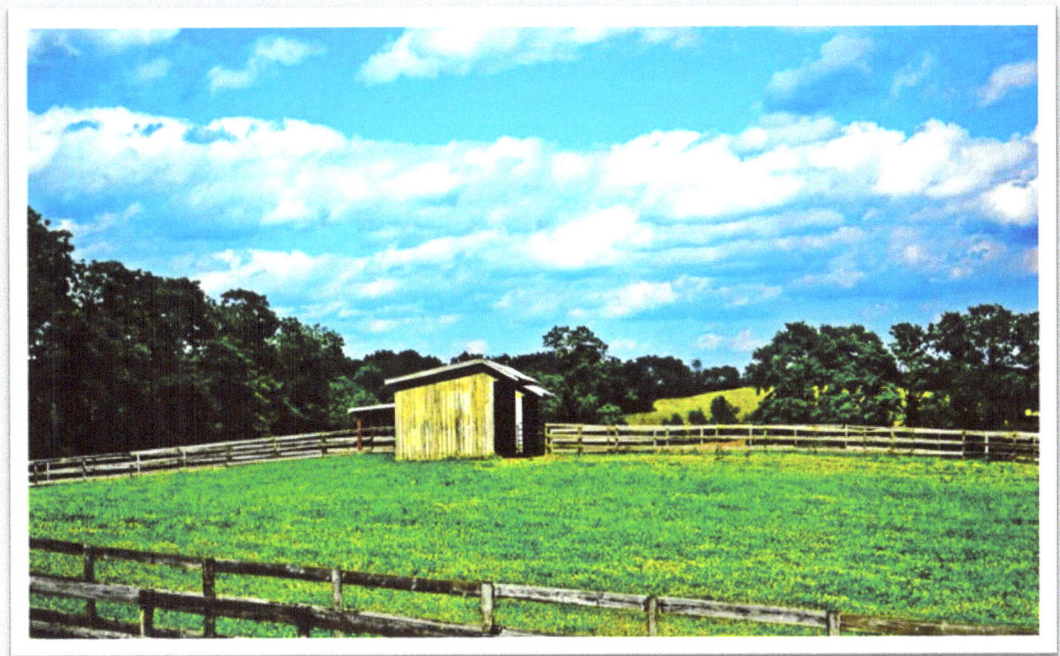

Ways in Which Digital is Inferior to Film:

Film is ultimately higher in resolution than digital. So, for making very large prints, film currently can't be beat. This is especially true for photos which have a lot of texture that needs to be preserved, such as landscapes.

Film produces a "first-generation" image in that it is a direct representation of the light that entered the camera, unlike digital.

These days, even very high-end film cameras are usually less expensive or the same cost as a new mid-range DSLR, and will not become obsolete in only a few years' time.

The dynamic range of film, which is its ability to retain details in highlights and shadows, is greater. Also, it is much more forgiving of overexposure and will not blow out the highlights nearly as much as digital will.

Film is more forgiving of subtle focusing issues.

You can double-expose film, which is something that the majority of digital cameras simply can't do.

Film cameras don't require nearly as much power to operate, so battery life is much longer than a digital camera.

Shutter lag is very slightly less than in digital cameras. This used to be a bigger issue than it is now.

While this is purely subjective, some photographers believe that film is a more "authentic" form of photography. However, the same line of thinking was prominent in the very early days of photography when painters complained that photography was lacking in creativity.

Ways in Which Film is Inferior to Digital:

Film simply takes much more work to create an image.

Prints from negatives are completely the result of the skills and tastes of the person making the print. Unless you have the facilities to make the prints yourself, you will almost always end up with a result that you didn't intend. This can basically ruin your image and render it useless to you. The exception to this is slide (transparency) film which is what most professional photographers once used.

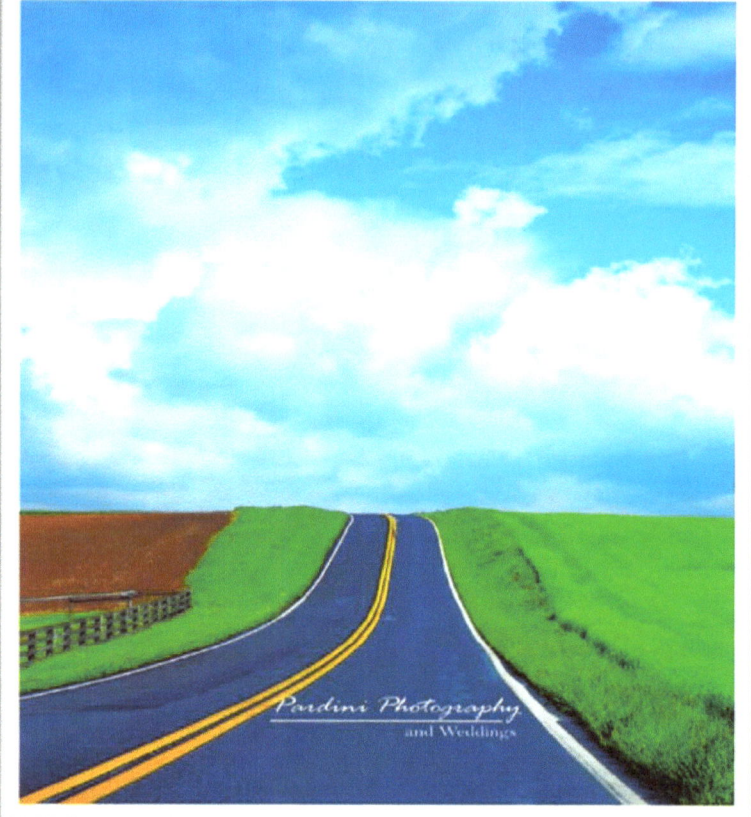

Storing negatives and prints, which all need to be laboriously hand-labeled, can end up taking up lots of space for the avid photographer.

While it is possible to scan film into your computer and edit your images in software like Photoshop, there will always be some loss of image quality. This is true even if the most expensive professional scanner is used.

While the initial cost of a film camera is indeed lower, the ongoing cost of buying and processing film will quickly add up to a very large expense.

No instant gratification. You must wait until the film is developed to see your photos. Can't tell you how many times I was on 'Pins and Needles' wait for my photos to return from the lab!

Digital photography, for most applications, is much more convenient. You can shoot hundreds, or even thousands, of images and make prints that are a few feet on a side. Also, In this day and age with so much of our work being shared electronically via email and online galleries, digital cameras are ideal. Digital cameras are usually lighter and a single memory card can store more photos than many rolls of film.

It is easy to import your photographs into image editing software such as Photoshop, and there will be no loss of image quality from using a scanner. This also makes it easy to only print the photos you want from a batch, rather than having to print and entire roll of film horrid shots and all.

Digital cameras are capable of higher speeds than film, so they perform better in low-light situations. Also, it is very easy to change speed on a digital camera whereas a film camera requires a completely new roll of film.

In conclusion, for very high quality images and prints (up to 11" x 14" or even higher with the use of some specialized software), a good digital camera system, in the right hands, and with

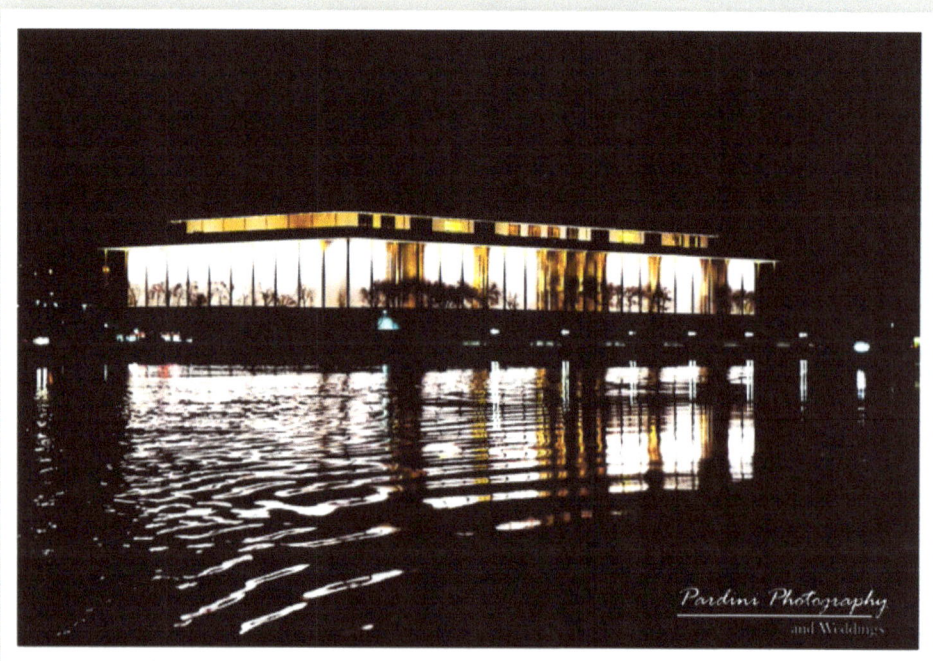

appropriate post-processing, is more than up to the job, and is the equal (or better) of 35mm film cameras. The advent of digital Single Lens Reflex (SLR) systems in the last year have enabled.

Photographers to use the same high quality lens systems used by professional film photographers on a digital body. To me, this gives the best of both worlds. And higher resolution/quality digital bodies will continue to be developed, so you can keep all the lenses and accessories, upgrade the camera back, and stay on the crest of the wave of cutting edge technology.

One last thing to consider….Neither film nor digital is ultimately "better." Each photographer must choose which photographic format that works for their application, budget and personal preferences. It is indeed ultimately the photographer and not the medium which defines what is quality. While the use of film has significantly declined due to the explosion of digital photography, it is certainly still has its uses and isn't going away anytime soon.

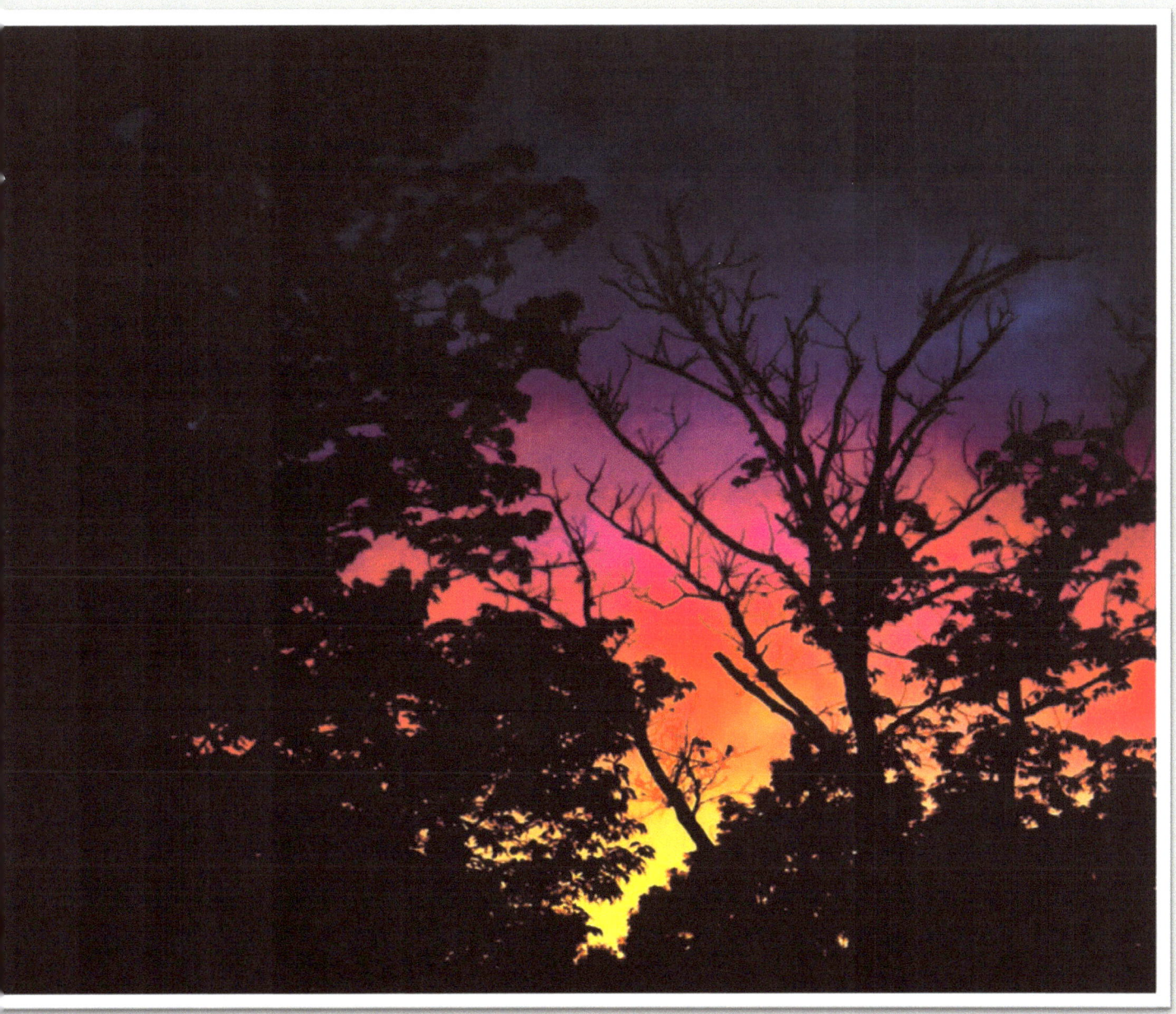

Difference Between Erasing and Formatting a Memory Card!

Majority of digital camera owners do not understand the difference between erasing and formatting a memory card.

Before explaining the differences, it should be pointed out that most memory card manufacturers recommend formatting a new memory card by the camera before using the card for the first time to setup the correct file system.

Erasing can be done whenever needed, such as when your card is at full capacity and you need more space on the card. You can erase all or individual image files.

A memory card should be formatted several times a year, particularly if its performance seems sluggish. Use your camera format tool to do this…

Before erasing or formatting a memory card, you should make certain that you backup all important images first!

Erasing a Memory Card: When erasing a memory card, individual image files are deleted from their directories on the card. You can erase one or more selected images at a time, or you can erase all images at one time. However, images that you selected to be "protected" through another menu option on the camera will not be removed during the erasure process.

Formatting a Memory Card: Formatting deletes all images from a memory card, even the ones that may have been protected. It recreates the file system that the camera needs, including new directories and folders where images are saved on the card. Most software that will allow you to restore images that were accidently deleted have better success restore rates on a freshly formatted memory card.

***Unlike erasing, formatting improves the overall performance of a card.

Use your camera to format, not your computer: Though opinions vary, many recommend formatting a memory card in a digital camera, not via a computer. If you plan to use a memory card that was previously used in another camera, format the card in the new camera before taking any shots. File directories/folders where the images save are different in each camera.

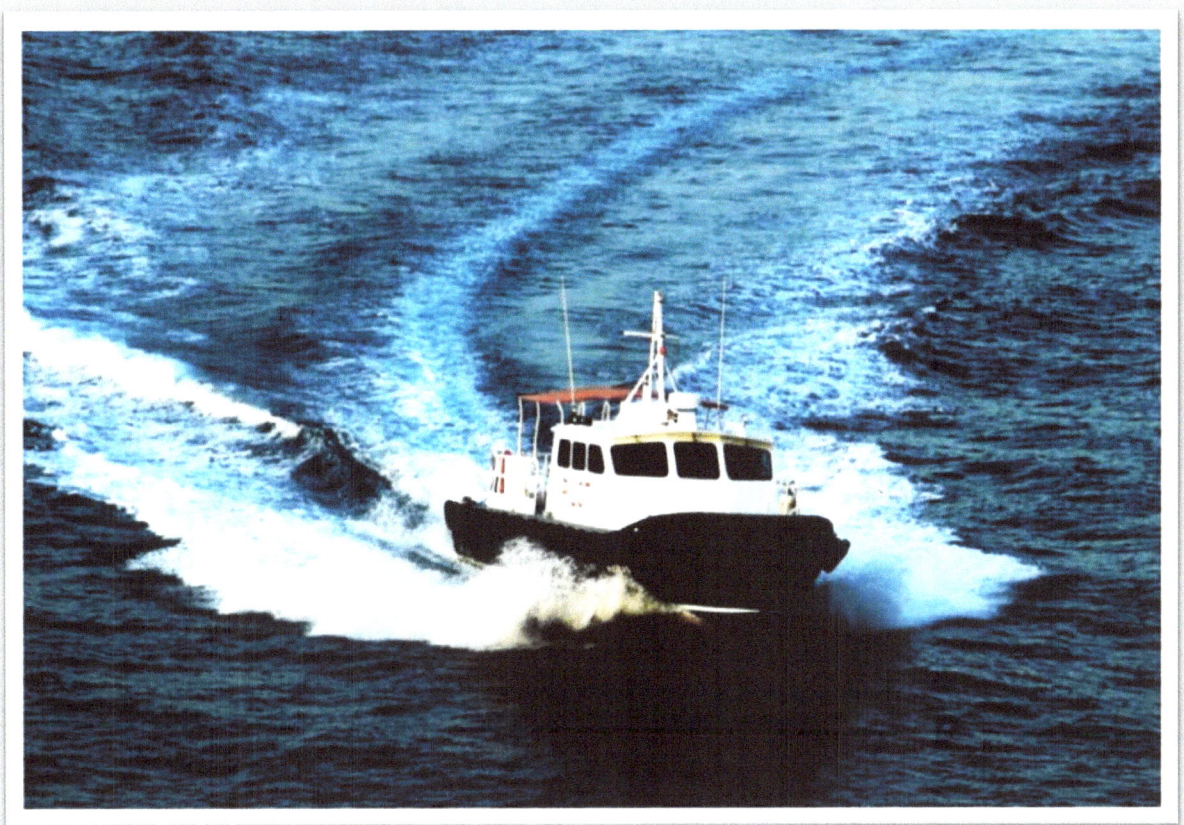

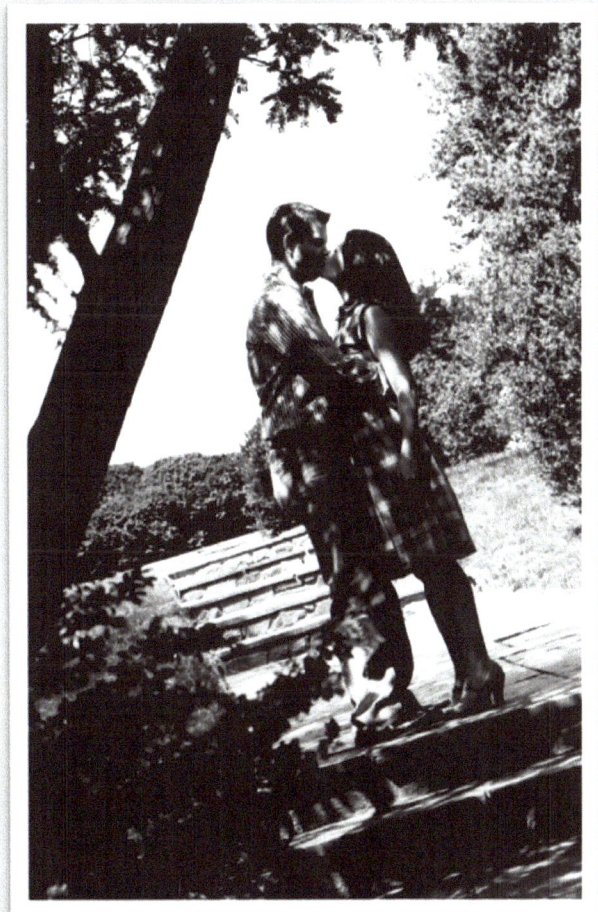

Framing Your Shots

We often put photographs and pictures in frames as a way of displaying them – but there is another type of framing that you can do when taking your shots that can be just as effective doing just the same thing…

Framing is the technique of drawing attention to the subject of your image by blocking other parts of the image with something in the scene…a foreground frame as you will!

<u>The Benefits of Framing Photographs Include:</u>

- Giving the photo composition (for example framing a scene with an archway can tell you something about the place you are by the architecture of the archway or including some foliage in the foreground of a shot can convey a sense of being out in nature).
- Giving images a sense of depth and different layers.
- Drawing your viewer's eyes towards the main focal point you are trying to show off.
- Intriguing your viewer. Sometimes it's what you can't see in an image that draws you into it as much as what you can see in the picture. Clever framing that leaves those viewing your image wondering a little or imagining what is behind your frame can be quite effective…
- Fames for photographs come in all shapes and sizes and can include shooting through overhanging branches, shooting through windows, using tunnels, arches or doorways – you can even use people (for example shooting over shoulders or between heads) etc.
- Your frame doesn't need to go completely around the edges of your image – they might just be on one or two edges of your shot.
- My general rule is when considering framing ask the question: 'will this add to or take away from the image?' Sometimes framing can just add clutter to a shot and make it feel cramped – but at other times it can be the difference between an ordinary shot and a stunning one.
- Lastly – if you do use framing techniques, you also need to consider whether you want your frame to be in focus or not. In some instances, a nicely blurred frame will really add a sense of mood and depth to your shots (in this case use a large aperture) but in other cases to have your frame in focus can help with adding context to the scene (in this case choose a narrow aperture).

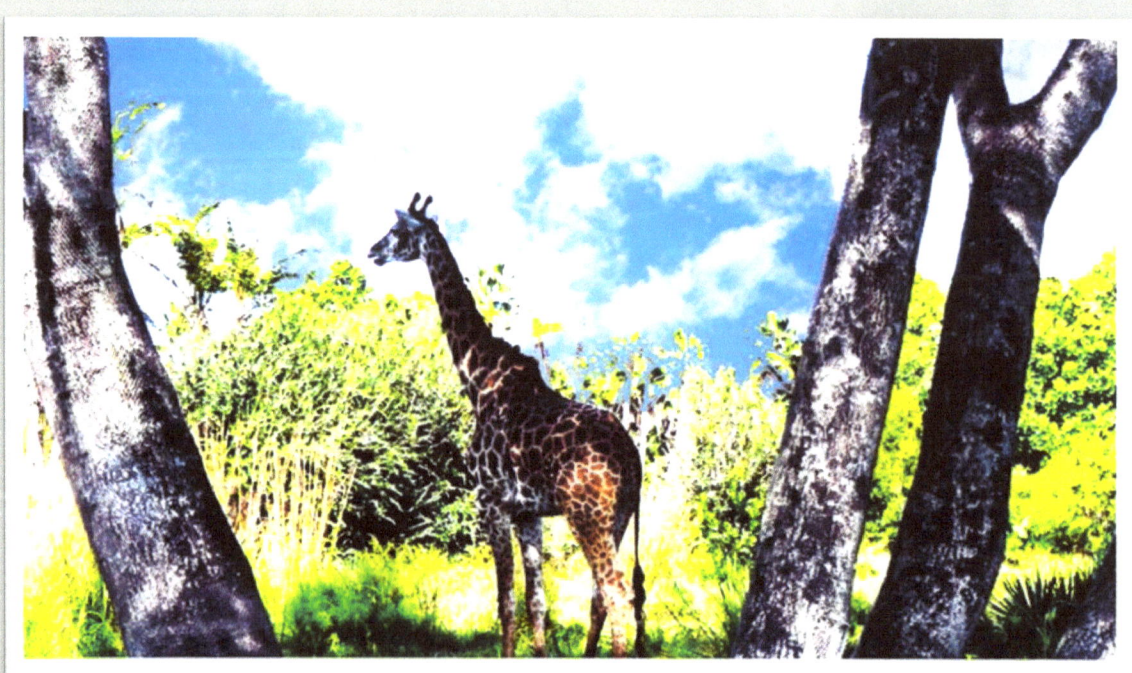

Shooting Halloween Photographs

Halloween is difficult to shoot because most of the photos will be taken in the dark and in low lighting conditions. In honor of Halloween, I wanted to put together (13) thirteen quick tips to help you take great Halloween photos so all of its festivities will come to its goulash glory in pictures. This article will also help you with some creative tips to help your Halloween photos stand out!

- Turn off your flash. The flash will brighten the subject you are shooting. It will also murder the Halloween atmosphere you are trying to capture.

- Setting a longer camera exposure will help to capture Halloween scenes in its creepy glory! Be careful and use a tripod or brace your camera because any movement in your shots will come out blurry. Sometimes blurriness can be a plus on adding a creepy flair to your shots.

- Make sure there is a little ambient light to capture Jack-o-Lanterns so not only the objects are visible but a little of the outside as well. The best Halloween photos could be taken at dusk when there's still enough natural light.

- Set a high ISO setting of 800 or higher. This is essential to capture spooky mood, dark colors of Halloween and ambient light if you don't use tripod. Plus you can use faster shutter speed. The downside is that you will get more noise in your photos. You can always fix the noise later with the help of Photoshop…

- To get a sharp shot of people in Halloween action you will need to rely on the flash.

- Diffusing the flash on your camera with colored cellophane – red or yellow – or secured with a rubber band wax paper will decrease the flash impact on your shot and instead of bold brightening will give a glow to your photo.

- Halloween scenes can be tricky to shoot because several light sources can be present such as candles, flash, street lighting. Florescent lights will give your picture a greenish tint, while incandescent bulbs will make your pictures golden yellow. Make sure that the white balance is set right.

- Place extra candles behind the pumpkins as well as inside them when taking photos to give a little extra light. This will help you to capture the full effect of the glowing inside the pumpkin.

- It is tricky to balance between overexposing and underexposing when shooting Halloween due to the light and dark patches in the scene. If you take a number of shots at different exposures or use exposure bracketing, you should get one or two that give you the impact you're after.

- Try to find new angles and look beyond the standard Jack-o-Lanterns. Look for new perspectives such as shooting the process of decorations, carving the pumpkin, people getting dressed in costumes, people holding lit pumpkins silhouetted against the sky at dusk can really pay off.

- Use candles for shooting not only Jack-o-Lantern but people in Halloween costumes as well. Candles give your photo anything from a romantic look to a chilling Halloween look. Try the classic candle below the mask. Have the subject hold the candle next to his/her body and get a spooky look. This will also add more shooting light.

- Getting in close and filling the frame with your subjects will usually add punch to your shots. Try to use a macro lens or the flower in option that most cameras have. Capture small details such as glowing fangs, glittery hair or your kid's made-up eyes.

- Have fun and Happy Halloween! While trying to take great looking Halloween photos, do not forget that it is a holiday and have fun too!

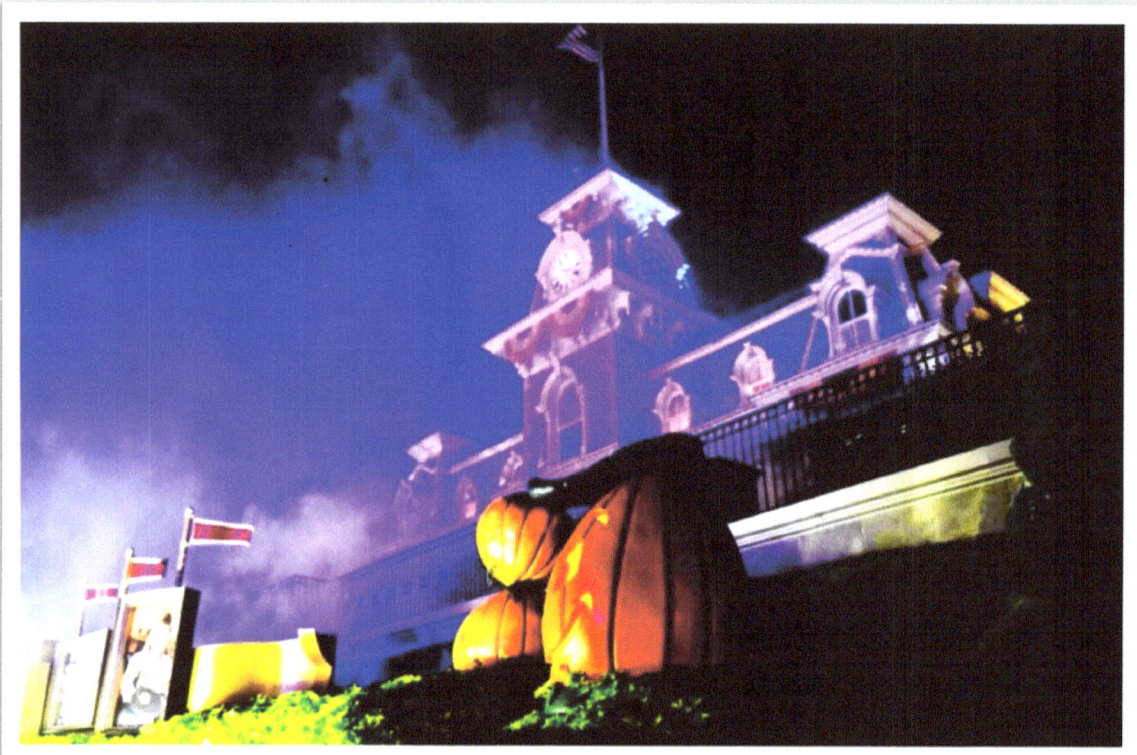

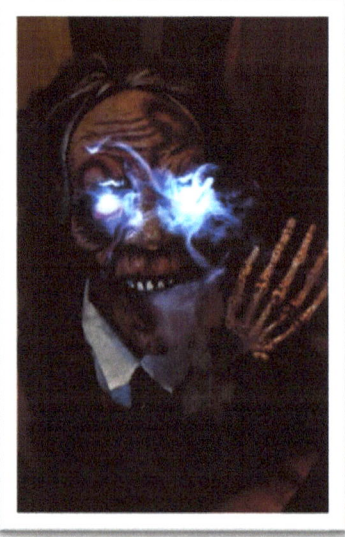

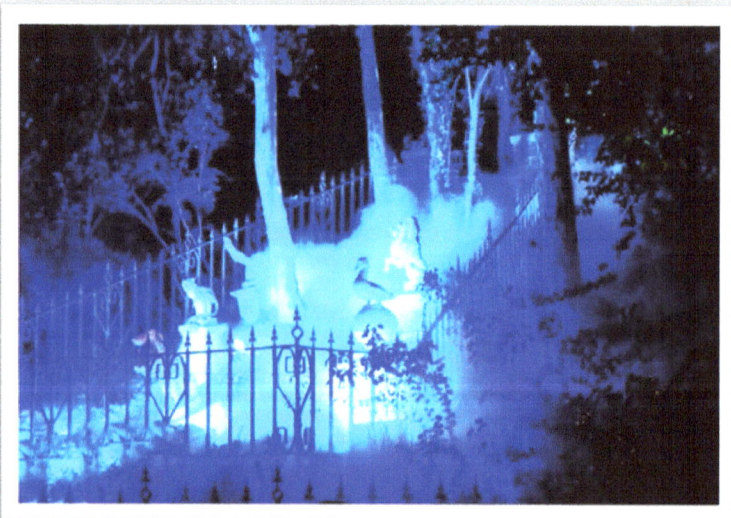

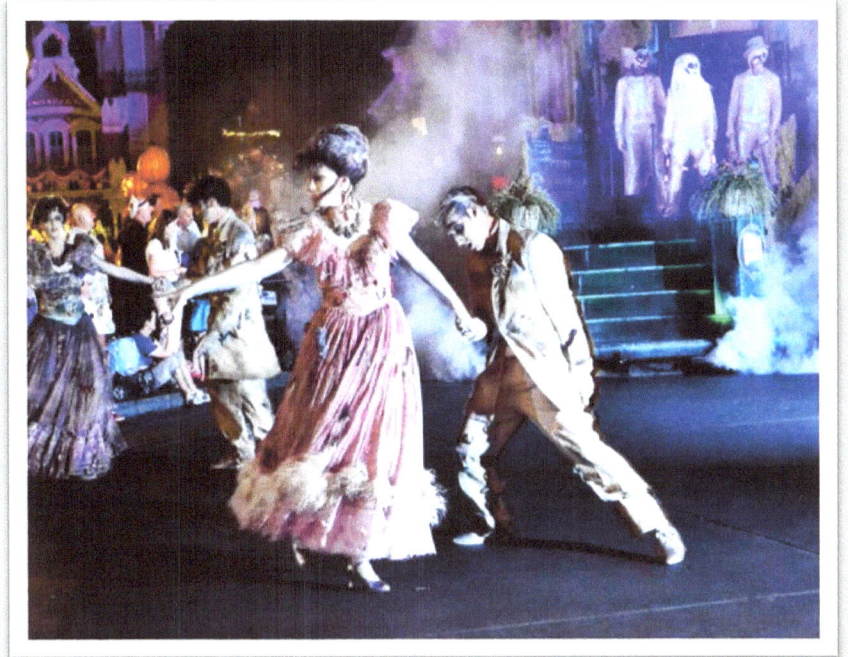
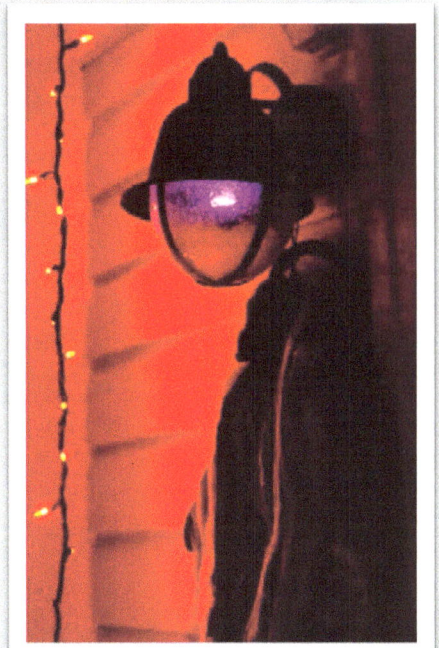

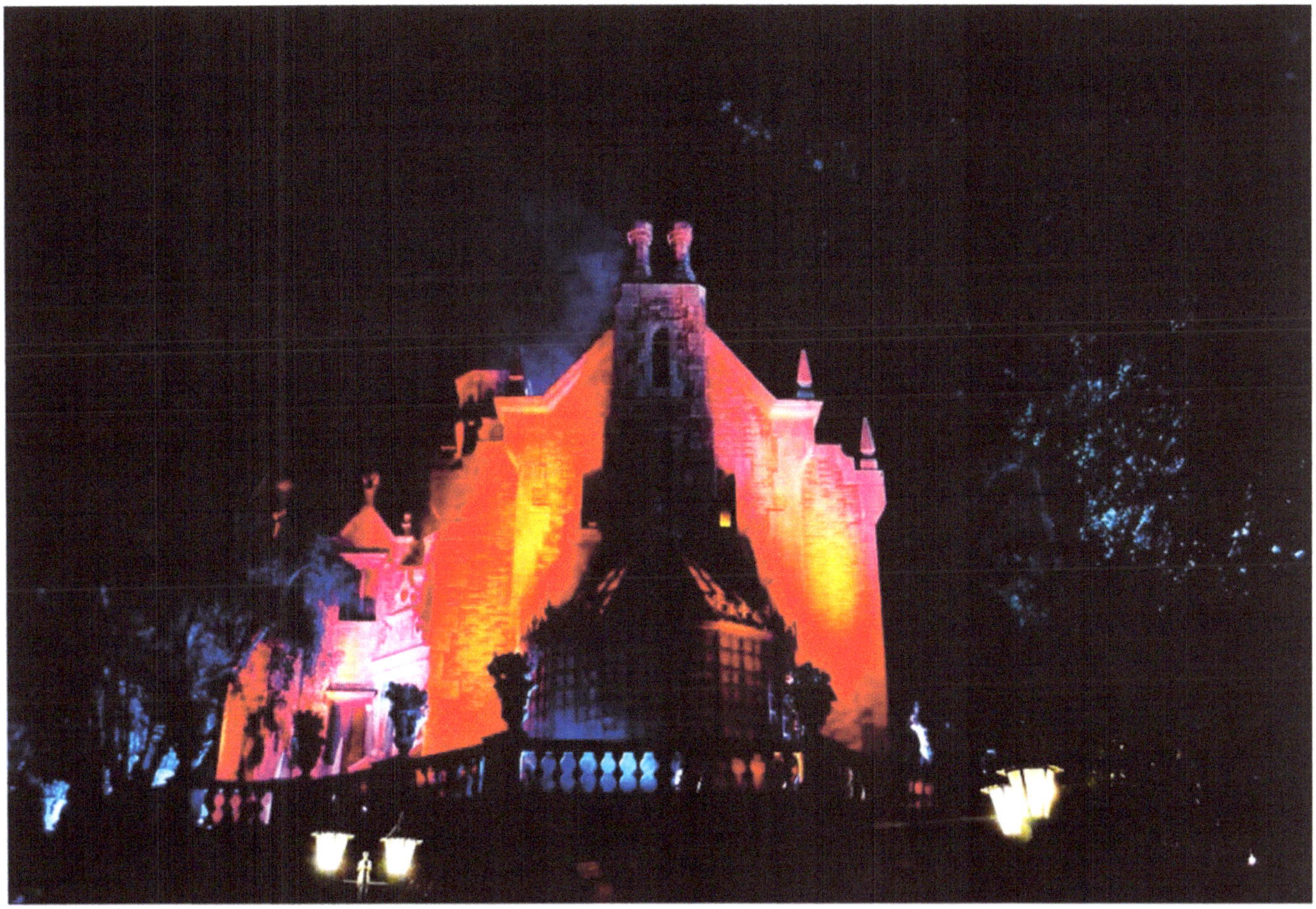

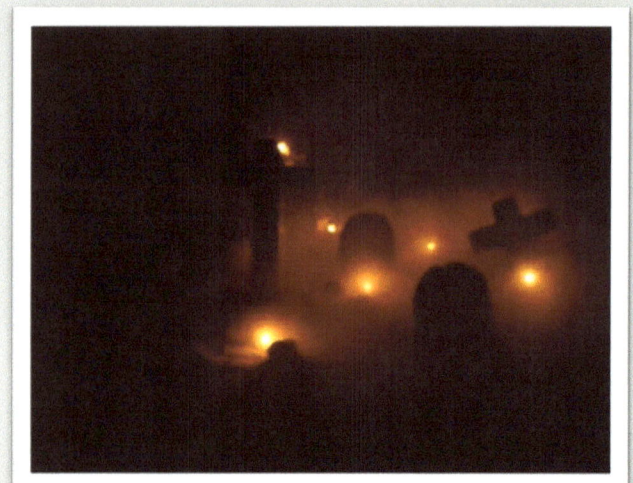
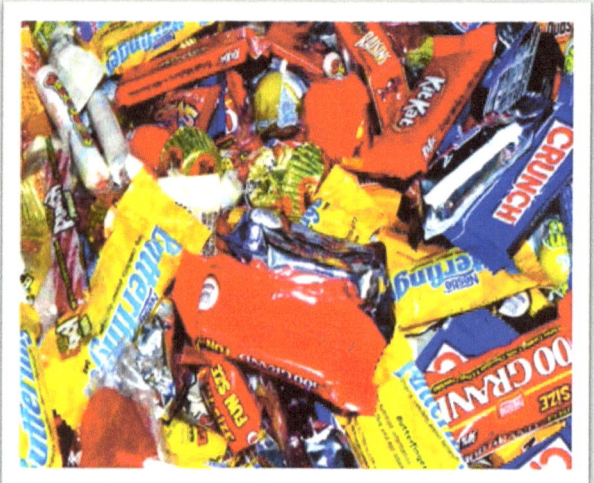
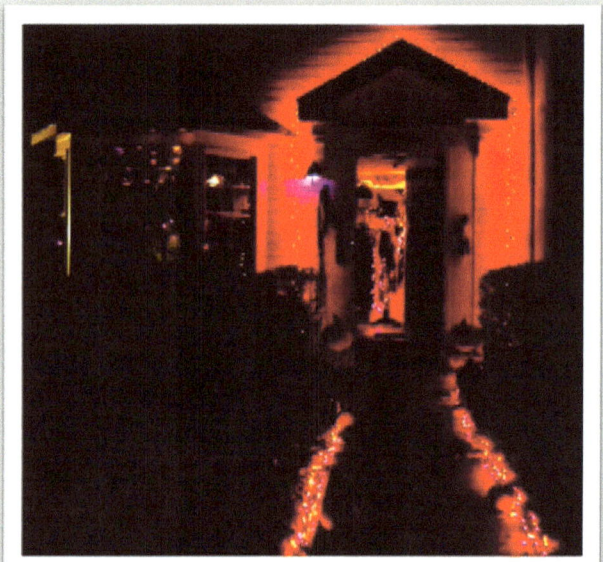
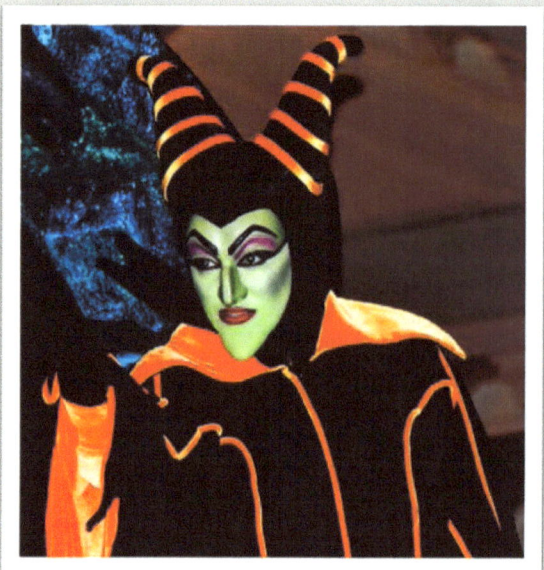
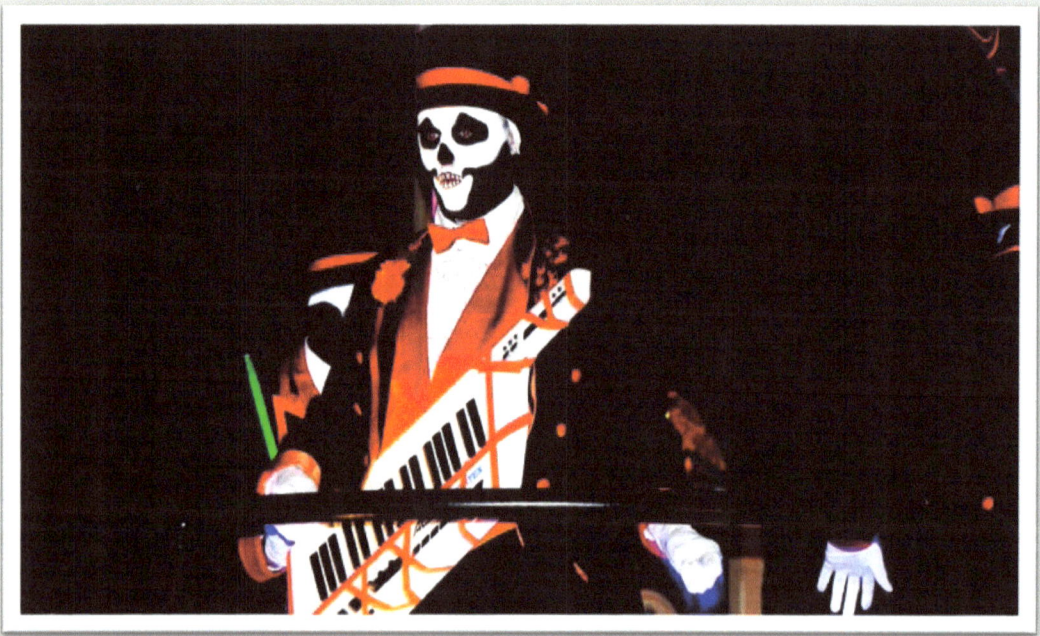

Memorial Day Photographs

Whatever your plans are - picnics, barbecues, road trips, parades, etc. - snap some pics!

Here's a few tips to remember: Change the angles: get up on a chair or get down on the ground. Changing your position relative to your subject can really give you some great shots and add a lot of composition! Sometimes this little technique can make a good photograph into art!

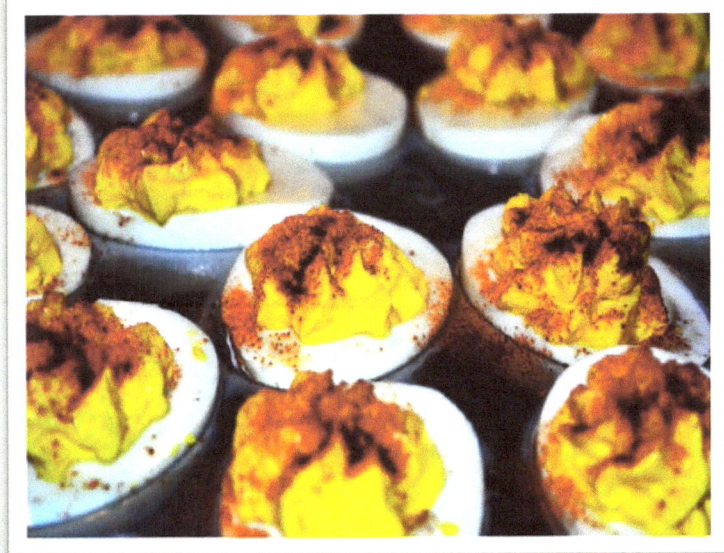

Get Close: fill the frame with your subject. Try out that macro setting on your camera for a new twist.

Be Candid: sometimes candid photos of friends and family are the best ones and shows the 'true' story of the day…Photojournalism if you will! Remember, we want to show the world what you see through your eyes of the moment!

Even everyday scenes and activities will have that impact! It is perfectly acceptable to edit your photos! In the new digital age, you have the chance to crop, rotate, color, enhance, add effects and sharpen photos on your computer using readily available software. Be creative and go for it! I will tell you this… most of today's fine photographic art is touched up in this way, so be creative and go for it!

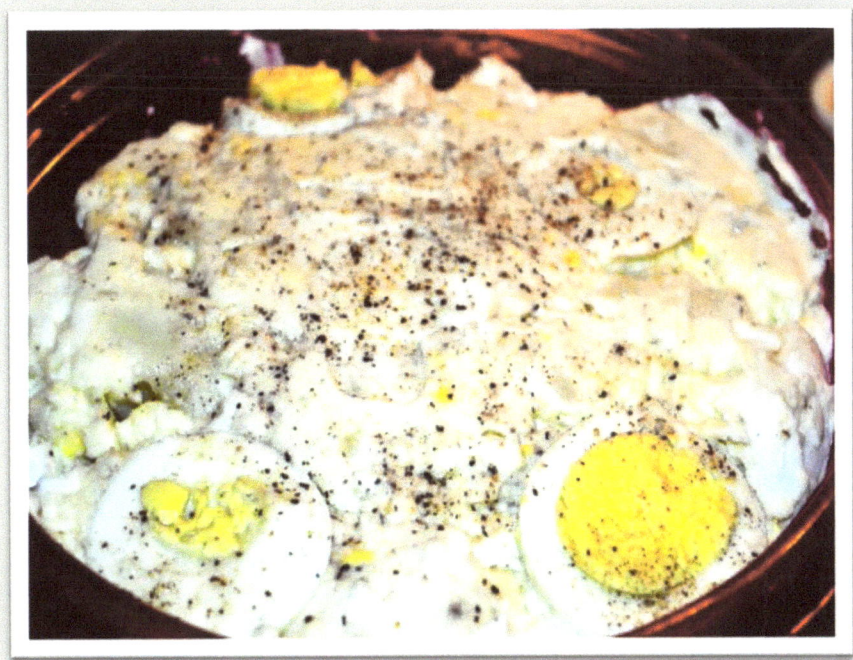

Quick Tips for Taking Excellent 'Fireworks' Photos

- Turn off your flash.

- Set the lens to manual focus and set it to the ∞ (infinity) mark. With most autofocus cameras, use autofocus to focus on something very far away, and then reset it to Manual focus to lock the focus at infinity for the rest of the night.

- If you can, put the camera on tripod. Use a cable release or remote control so you won't have to jiggle the camera.

- If you don't use a tripod, the smooth streaks will become squiggles. If you want weird special effects, be my guest and wiggle the camera around to see what happens.

- If your camera has it, shoot on M or Manual exposure mode.

- Set the camera on "B" or "Bulb." When you press the shutter, the camera opens to light, and stays open until you remove your finger.

- Some cameras have a "T" (time) setting, which instead stays open by itself and closes when you press the shutter a second time. This isn't as convenient.

- If you have neither of these, set a long manual exposure of many seconds, and start the exposure the usual way. Use your hand in front of the lens to stop it. If you have no remote control or cable release, set a long exposure and use your hand or a hat to start and stop the exposure.

- If you have none of these settings, so long as you turn off your flash, you will be as good to go as possible.

- Shoot at the lowest ISO for the best results. Turn off ISO AUTO because it will try to set a high ISO in the dark. If you have no idea what ISO is, forget about it.

- Try an aperture of f/5.6 at ISO 50 and ISO 100, and f/8 at ISO 200 for starters. If you don't know what an aperture is, or your camera doesn't have this adjustment, don't worry.

- Open the shutter before the first burst. Hold it open several seconds, until one burst completes, or hold it open longer for several bursts.

- As more bursts happen, they "draw" on you film or digital, and add together to look like they all happened at once. If you only open the shutter for one burst, you get one. If you hold it open for several consecutive bursts, you'll get a photo loaded with all of them.

- How does it look? Too dark? Open up the aperture (set more towards f/4). Is it too washed-out? Stop down (towards f/11). Try again until you get an exposure you like, at whatever aperture you need.

- The brightness of the burst depends only on ISO and the aperture (f/stop). They don't vary with the amount of time the shutter is open.

- The brightness of the sky, but not the bursts, also varies with the length of the exposure.

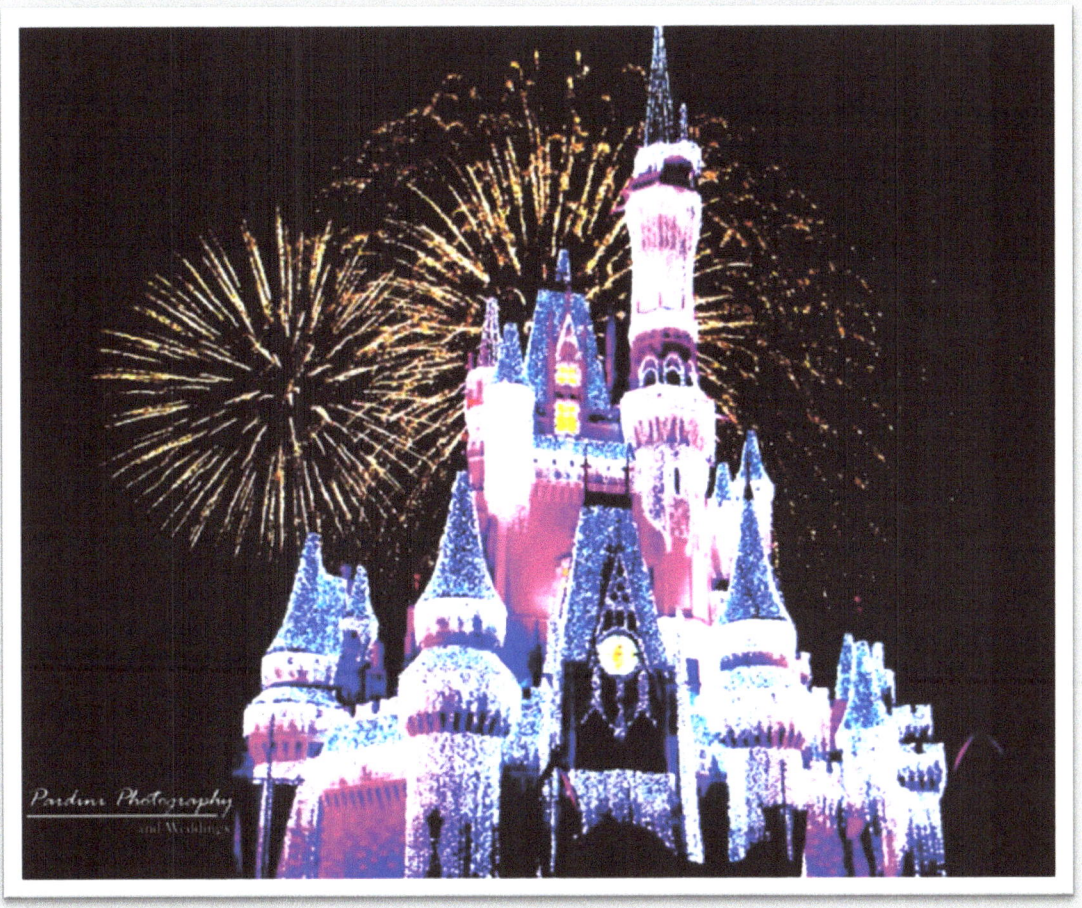

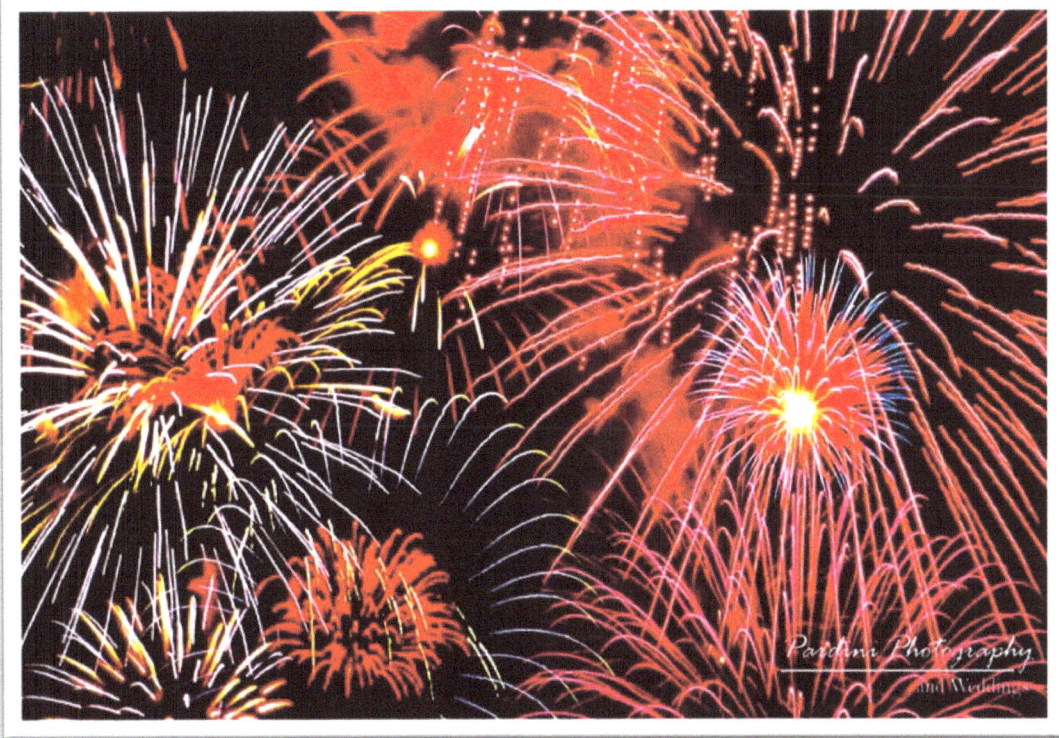

How to Shoot Group Portraits Indoors

If you are photographing a large group and you do not know what you are doing, it will become obvious very quickly! People will become inpatient, which could make for a not so great photograph! To avoid hearing some harsh words or getting a large group frustrated quickly, learn the basic steps of the process so you will be prepared!

Check out the venue prior to determine the best location for the group photograph! You can also do some research online to see if there were other group photographs taken at that same location and what looked good and what did not… Try to find an area where the background is not distracting to draw the viewers of the photograph to the subjects and not random objects in the frame. Ensure that the faces of all of the people are visible!!! I always like to tell everyone 'if you cannot see me and my camera…the camera cannot see you and you will be cut out of the photograph!'

Look through the lens and compose the photograph so that the subjects fill the frame.

Set the aperture correctly for how many people are in the shot. Greater numbers of people in a group will require a narrower aperture to keep everyone in focus maintaining a greater depth of field. An aperture of f/16 should suffice for a large group with 20 or more, but it does not hurt to go even narrower to a setting like f/22. For smaller groups of 6 to 8 people, f/8 will be a good starting point. Always take a few seconds to review your shots after you set the aperture to see if everyone is in focus. This is a good time to use aperture bracketing…

Use a swiveling external flash to achieve softer lighting in group portraits. Turn the swiveling head upward and slightly backward to bounce the light off of the wall and ceiling. If the bounced light form the flash is not bright enough, set the ISO incrementally higher until you reach the desired exposure. But do not go too high so prevent noise!

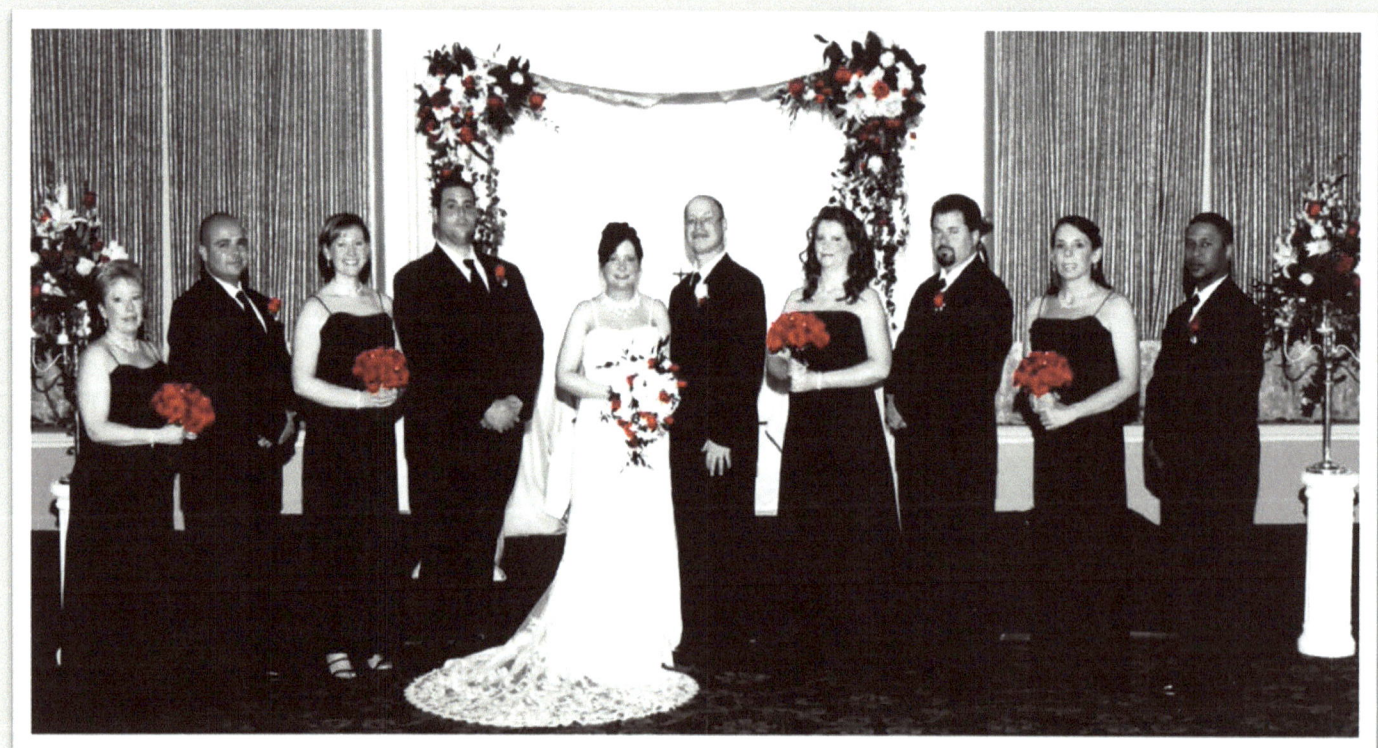

Low Light and Nighttime Photography

Photography in dim/low lighting can be used to create interesting and amazing photos. When I say photography at night, I mean dim to total darkness. The long exposures associated with low light can create unique effects and unusually sharp photos. And when I say long exposures, I mean exposures lasting from 1/25 seconds up to even 30 seconds. An exposure that long would seem impossible to prevent shaking, so my technique that I use very often is to compose the photo like I would normally and then to set the self-timer so the camera takes the picture on its own and I don't even have to touch it.

Equipment:

For low light photos, a tripod (or some kind of substitute) is necessary. I almost always keep a tripod with me on most photo shoots and trips… A miniature tripod can be very handy because it is typically small enough to fit in a pants pocket so it can be taken anywhere. Some photographers carry around a bean bag or something like it so that can set their camera down and tilt it in any way they like. Some of my best pictures I have taken simply by setting my camera down on a table, flat surface, roof of my car, etc. and setting the self-timer.

Many photographers are convinced that they need a cable release to take long exposures, however, the self-timer option on just about all cameras works just as good! All you have to do is configure the self-timer, press the shutter button, and wait the 10 seconds and the camera will take the photo automatically. And you don't have to touch the camera so the photo won't be blurred from hand shaking.

Opportunities:

Adding some kind of foreground item to the frame helps to create a greater depth of field, this technique works for any kind of photo, but I have found that it makes night landscape photos much better. Another tip you should keep in mind is that the main subject of a night photo should probably be the best lit. Lots of light is good for a night exposure, but there should still be some focus applied to the major objects in a scene. Another easy tip is to focus in on the brightest part of the subject and the camera will meter off it.

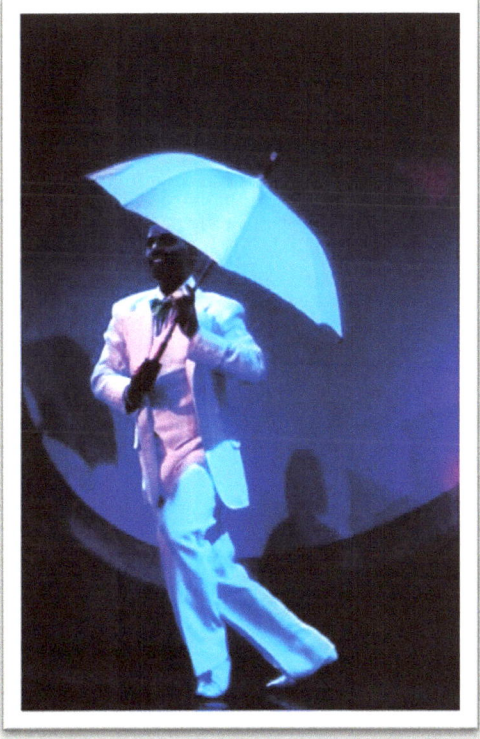

Technical:

When taking photos at night, you should keep aperture in mind as well as shutter speed. It is without question that you will need a long shutter speed, but the aperture that you choose will provide the depth of field. When I take night photos, I usually have a very long shutter speed (5-15 seconds) and a very narrow aperture (high f-stop). This combination creates a huge depth of field and makes everything very crisp and in focus. Of course, sometimes you will not desire a great depth of field and in those situations you should widen the aperture (small f-stop).

It is also recommended to use a high ISO setting. Some cameras will add noise (grain) when the ISO is higher and most of the newer cameras will reduce the noise creating a cleaner crisp photograph.

Calculating the Exposure:
Figuring out what exact shutter speed and aperture, you should use can be very challenging in Manual Mode. I would recommend that you just try many different combinations for each scene and eventually you will refine the settings that you prefer. Another technique I use is bracketing, if you bracket all your photos so the camera takes multiple exposures at different settings, you are more likely to end up with a photo that has a satisfactory brightness.

Conclusion:
There is no exact science to dim/low light photography; I hope some of these tips will guide you in the right direction. But the best night photographers are usually the people who experiment a lot when they are taking low light exposures and eventually they figure out the best scenes and best exposure settings to match. Just remember that you need a very long shutter speed setting, and that you need to keep the camera very steady. Take lots of photographs and have fun!

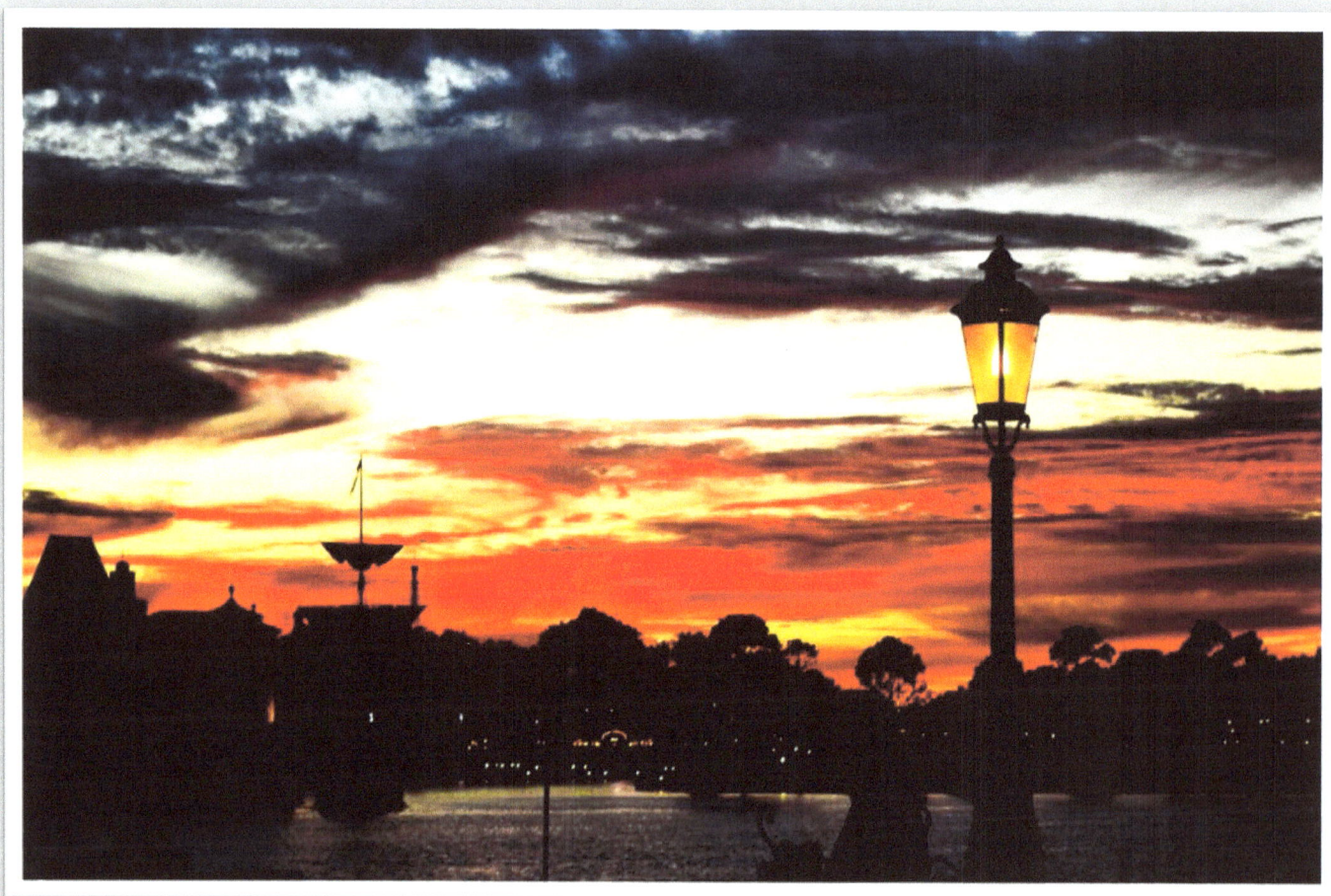

Taking Control of Digital Noise When Shooting at High ISO Sensitivity

Noise in digital photography is the same as what we use to call grain in film photography… This is typically caused by shooting at a high ISO setting, usually greater than 800. Without going too far into explaining noise, it is to say that it relates to how the individual pixels in your camera's sensor convert the light striking the sensor into electrical signals, which the image processor "processes" to create the resulting image.

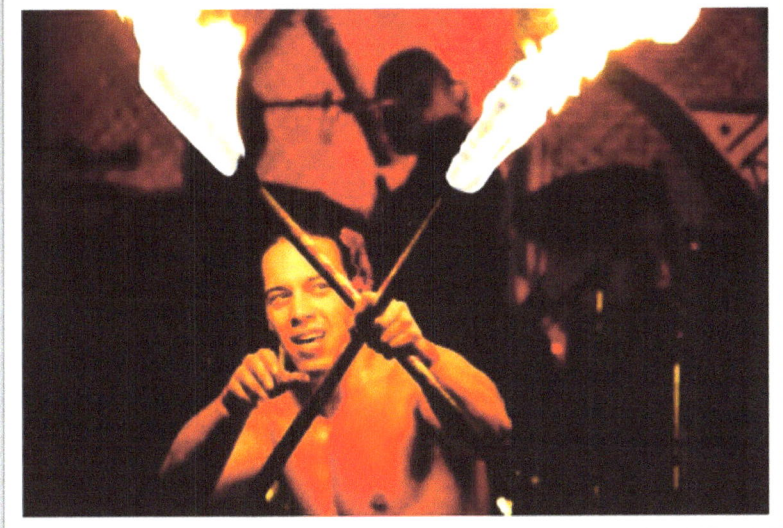

Typically, you increase the ISO sensitivity to more than 800 when the light is low and you do not want to use a flash, or you're shooting where it is not allowed. Shooting conditions may also make it necessary to shoot at a faster shutter speed to stop action, such as indoor sports: basketball, hockey, etc., which is another reason you might hike the ISO to achieve a proper exposure and sharp image. Holding your camera at a slower shutter speed in low light could cause camera shake and blurred images. The solution is often a tripod, but not all shooting situations make it practical to use a tripod, as you must be on the move to capture your photos.

For two primary reasons, noise is not necessarily a condition to avoid.

- If you expect to generate sharp, properly exposed photos, especially if you're a professional on a shoot, then you may have to be willing to allow for some visible noise. Again, you may not have an alternative if you don't happen to have a flash unit with you or you're not permitted to interrupt a sporting event, concert or a speech with the light from a flash. Many of the better wedding photographers purposely don't use a flash, so they can work close to their subjects without blasting a light in their faces or adding shadows to the photos.
- Once you understand digital noise and how it occurs, you can control it and use it as a creative element. Noise could help to emphasize textures or give a photograph grittiness, if, for example, you shoot many street and urban scenes and subject matter.

Fortunately, the technology of digital photography also provides methods to eliminate or reduce noise that weren't available to film photographers...

- Virtually all of the newest DSLR cameras, from low priced entry levels to the most expensive professional cameras, have been engineered with advanced technology to control digital noise. This technology is also found in the newer interchangeable lens camera systems, or mirror less cameras, and many of the high-end compact cameras.
- The other advantage digital photography has over film photography for controlling noise is what can be done with noise reduction software compared to the limited methods of the darkroom such as the reduce noise feature in Photoshop.

- Like any digital photography concept, once you make noise part of your knowledge set, there is no reason to be afraid of its effect and, in fact, your use of it creatively is a sign that your skills are advancing and you have more control of the shooting process.

Pet Photography

Whether they're cute or ferocious, you want to immortalize your family pet on film. Don't worry if your Beagle, Siamese, or Iguana is camera shy, these little devils can't escape!

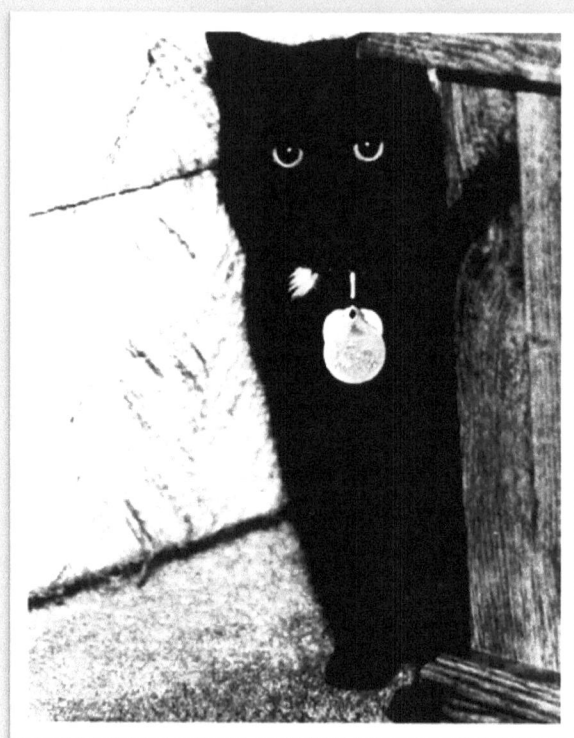

Get Inside Your Pet's Brain:

For a portrait, you want your four-legged buddy to feel at ease, so why not try to contain him or her in their favorite hangout…be it the rocking chair on the front porch, the stoop, on top of the fridge, or on top of your desk. Many cats like to rest on top of reading material, not for the intellectual stimulation, but to prevent their masters from reading so that they can get all the attention.

You should always respect your pet's personality when taking a photo just as you would for a human subject.   Chances are, though, if you dress your Saint Bernard up in red raincoat and booties, you're not going to get a natural expression.

Thou Shalt Tell A Story:

See a cat behind the table looking out? You can imagine the story behind this photo. It is a look that cat owners will recognize – that hypnotic stare that a cat gets when it intently studies a feathered object that it would like to nibble on. Next time you see a photo of a pet; see if it tells a story. It doesn't have to be a long story. It can be a short story as in this poodle in the pink tutu. Let's say you're trying to take a photo of your golden retriever and in walks your toddler with an ice cream cone and your golden retriever then knocks the cone out of his hands. The end result will be a photo that speaks for itself!

It's a good idea to have your camera at a central location in your home so you can grab it the second you see an animal story.

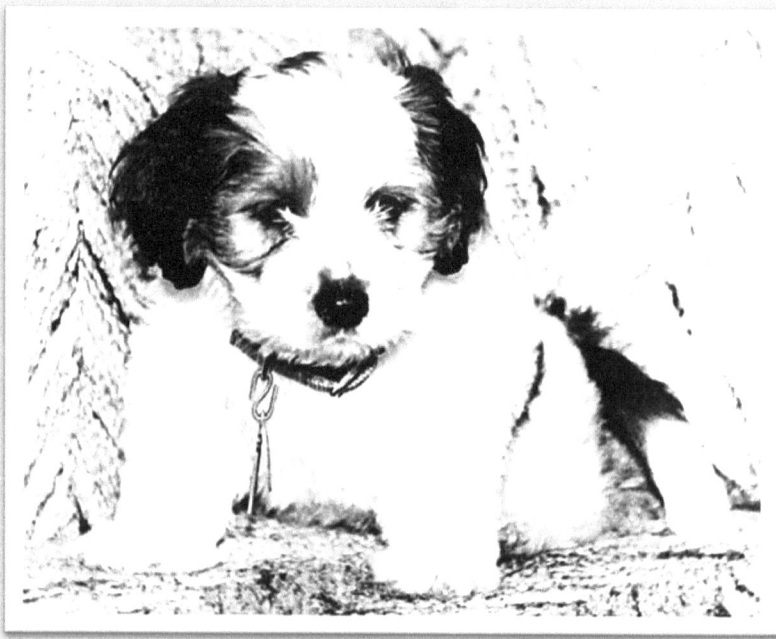

Be Prepared for Sudden Movement:

Pets can be unpredictable and move without warning. Consider your photo session a jungle safari of sorts and prepare for the cheetah's sudden escape. Sometimes pets can be restless and jump at the sound of a shutter click, so you should adjust your camera accordingly. Set your shutter speed at about 1/125th so your little cutie doesn't come across as one big orange fuzz ball. With film use a high speed such as ISO 400 or 800 film if you are going to be photographing indoors with minimal available light.

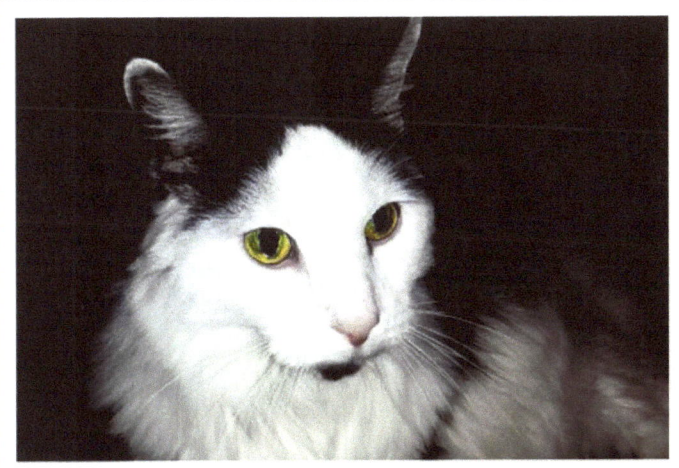

Consider your Camera Angle:

It's a good idea to place the camera at about the same level of the animal. This will fill your frame with your furry subject. If you're outdoors and your subject is digging for treasures or eating your neighbor's tulips, get down in the dirt so you can be at the same level. Seeing the subject's point of view, can give you an extra creative spark which will lead to better photographs.

If you are aiming for a glamorous close-up shot, you will want to use a close-up lens and be very quiet so you don't interrupt kitty's trance.

Don't Forget the Treats and the Props:

Treats are tools of the trade in pet photography. If you know your pet has a weakness for...say carrot cake, tuna, or Doritos, do not be afraid to use these to help you take that unforgettable shot. This can work especially well when photographing people with pets. (Though, you may want to get your vet's approval for the peanut butter.)

Study your Pet During the Day:

What sets her apart from other animals? What weird habits does she have? Some cats like to wrestle with stuffed animals, chase flies, and lick the spaghetti pot. If you want to take a funny photograph, the key is in the behavior. Aside from their life of luxury (sleeping, chasing ghosts and shadows, and eating), what do they do to entertain themselves? Do they adopt the same habits and patterns of behavior as their master's?

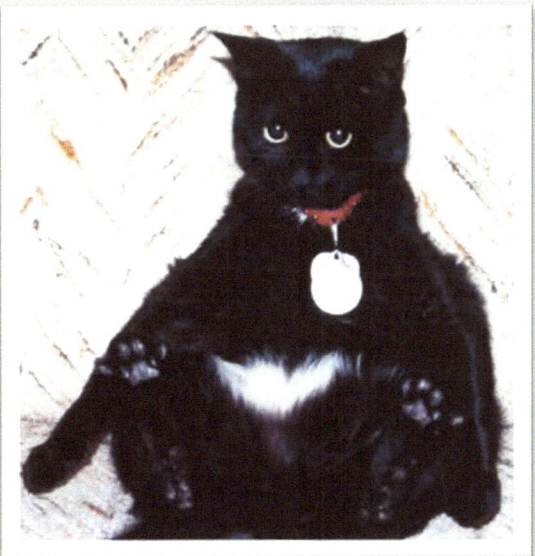

Rain Photography

To the naked eye, a rainy day or thunderstorm can be a beautiful event. But when you want to preserve that rain with a photograph, the result is typically an out-of-focus mess... There are a few things you can do to take good photographs of the rain.

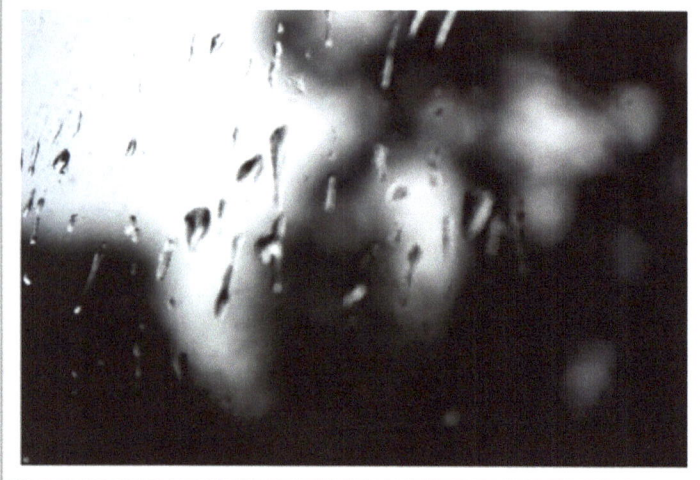

Get outside- Photos taken from inside through a window will not look sharp and in focus. You might get a little wet, but the difference in photo quality will be well worth it. Or open a window and lean out.

Use a tripod or support. You will want to get your photographs as in focus as possible and using a tripod will give you the most control. If you do not have a tripod, try using another flat surface that will hold your camera as still as possible.

Remember that just like any other action shot, the rain is moving and no matter what, so some of your rain will be blurry.

Compose your shot to get as much as you can of the foreground in focus, even if the background is completely out of focus.

Keep your camera covered at all times. Water can seriously damage your camera, so even if you are outside stay under an awning or if one is not available, cover yourself and your camera with a microfiber towel.

Be creative with how you take your rain photographs. It is not necessary to point and shoot into the air to watch the rain fall. Try different angles to get a fresh perspective that will take a more meaningful picture.

Consider photographing the splash of rain onto surfaces,

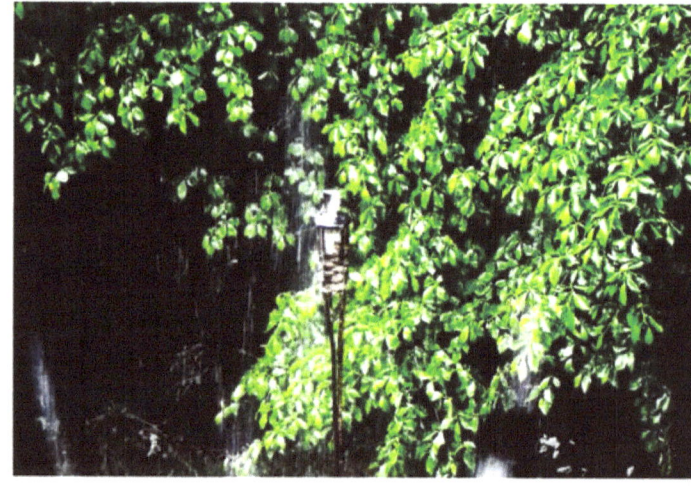

people playing in the rain, or the water as it beads off trees. Whatever you do, keep your eyes peeled for new and interesting ways to get your best rain shot.

Do not be afraid to get a little wet. It may dedication, but you will find that staying to get the right picture will make all of the difference.

A good rule of camera settings for rain is a 1/30 – 1/50 sec shutter speed, f5 – f5.6 and an ISO of 100 should do the trick….

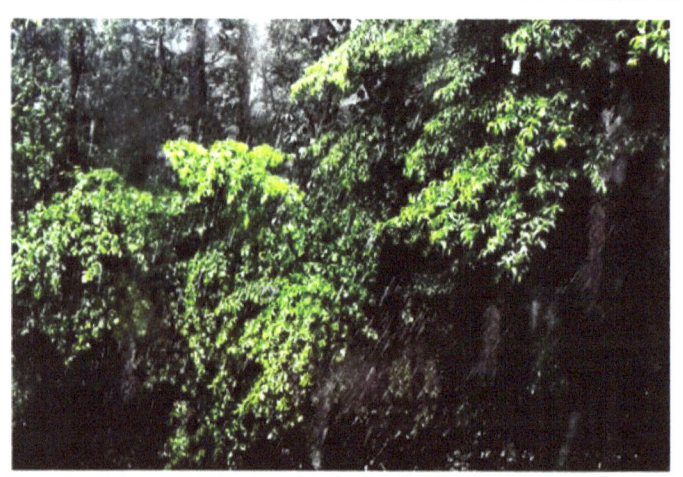

Should you Buy a DSLR or Point and Shoot Digital Camera?

DSLR:

- **DSLR is defined as:** *(Digital Single Lens Reflex)* Cameras that have removable lenses and have a reflex mirror which allows live optical viewing through the lens taking the image. E.G. DSLR's use a mirror that allows you to see the image you're about to shoot through the view finder when you take the shot, the mirror flips up allowing the image sensor to capture the image.

DSLR Strengths:

- *Image Quality* - due to the larger size of image sensors in DSLRs which allows for larger pixel sizes, DSLRs are generally able to be used at a faster ISO which will lead to faster shutter speeds and less grain / noise.
- *Adaptability* – DSLR's ability to change lenses opens up a world of possibilities for photographers. While my point and shoot has a nice little 3.6x Optical Zoom (and many these days have longer ones) my DSLR can be fitted with many high quality lenses ranging from wide angle, to zoom, to macro, depending what I am photographing. Add to this a large range of other accessories such as flashes, off camera flash bracket, filters etc. and a DSLR can be adapted to many different situations. It should be noted that when it comes to lenses, that the diversity in quality of lenses is great. Image quality is impacted greatly by the quality of the lens you use.
- *Speed* – DSLR's are generally pretty fast pieces of machinery when it comes to things like start up, focusing and fast shutter lag.
- *Optical Viewfinder* – due to the reflex mirror, DSLR's are very much, 'what you see…is what you get.'
- *large ISO range* - this varies between cameras, but generally, DSLRs offer a wide array of ISO settings which lends itself to their flexibility in shooting in different conditions...
- *Manual Controls* – while many point and shoots come with the ability to shoot in manual mode, a DSLR is designed in such a way that it is assumed that the photographer using it will want to control their own settings. While they do come with good auto modes, the manual controls are generally built in, in such a way that they are at the photographer's fingertips as they are shooting.
- *Depth of Field* – one of the things I love about my DSLR is the versatility that it gives me in many areas, especially depth of field. I guess this is really an extension of its manual controls and ability to use a variety of lenses, but a DSLR can give you depth of field that puts everything from foreground to background in focus through to nice blurry backgrounds.
- *Bracketing* – Some of the higher end DSLRs offer a Bracketing Feature. Bracketing is defined as the general technique of taking several shots of the same subject using different or the same camera settings while taking one photograph. Bracketing is useful and often recommended in situations that make it difficult to obtain a satisfactory image with a single shot, especially when a small variation in exposure parameters has a comparatively large effect on the resulting image.

DSLR Weaknesses:

- *Price* – while they are coming down in price (especially at the lower end) DSLR's are generally more expensive than point and shoot digital cameras. Also consider that you might want to upgrade your lens (as kit lenses are generally not of a super high quality) or you may wish to add more lenses later and that this adds to the cost of a DSLR.

- *Size and Weight* – the only reason I take my point and shoot with me is on those occasions when I don't want to lug my DSLR (and its lenses and flash) around with me. DSLRs are heavy and sizable and when you add a lens or two to your kit bag, you can end up with quite the load!

- *Maintenance* – a factor well worth considering if you're going to use a DSLR with more than one lens, is that every time you change lenses, you run the risk of letting dust into your camera. Dust on an image sensor is a real annoyance as it will leave your images looking blotchy. Cleaning your image sensor is not a job for the faint hearted and most recommend that you get it done professionally (which of course costs). This is a problem that is being rectified in many new DSLRs which are being released with self-cleaning sensors.

- *Noise* – DSLRs are generally noisier to use than point and shoots. This will vary depending upon the lens you use but while point and shoots can be almost silent when taking a shot, a DSLR will generally have a 'clunk' as the mechanisms inside it do their thing. I personally like this sound – but it's something that is a factor for some.

- *Complexity* – while DSLRs are designed for manual use, this of course means you need to know how to use the tools that they give you. Some friends that have bought DSLRs in the past have told me that they were a little overwhelmed at first by the array of settings and features. The learning curve can be pretty steep. Having said this – all DSLRs have fully automatic mode and many had the normal array of semi-auto modes that point and shoot digital cameras have and make normal picture taking easy as pie.

- *No live LCD* – in many DSLRs the only way to frame your shot is via the optical viewfinder. Some photographers prefer to use a camera's LCD for this task. This is another thing that is changing with more and more new DSLRs having a 'Live View' LCD which enables you to frame your shots without looking through the view finder.

So what <u>DSLR Do I Recommend?</u>

- It depends on your budget! I run a Nikon house and will only recommend Nikons... However, Canon does offer a nice camera too. You can look at it as: a Nikon is like a PC…where a Canon is like a MAC! And by surprise, most of the photographers I know that owns a Nikon uses a PC, and ones that own a Canon, uses a MAC! However, this is only about an 85% margin of truth… A decent low-end Nikon DSLR: D3100 MSRP: $650.00. A decent mid-range Nikon DSLR: D7000 MSRP: $1,200.00. A top of the line PRO Nikon DSLR: D3X MSRP $8,000.00. There are also medium format digital cameras that cost between $10,-30,000.

<u>Point and Shoot:</u>

- ***Point and Shoot*** is defined as a compact camera and designed primarily for simple operation. While some people write off all non DSLR's as not so nice, I think they've got a lot going for them and would highly recommend them depending upon the level of photography that you engage in, your budget, the things that you will want to do with your photographs and the subject matter that you will be shooting. Here's some Pros and Cons of point and shoot digital cameras:

<u>Point and Shoot Digital Camera Strengths:</u>

- *Size and Weight* - to be able to slip a camera in a pocket as you dash out the door to a party or a trip is a wonderful thing. These days point and shoot cameras can be slim and light – to the point of not even knowing you've got them with you. This is great for parties, travel and all situations.

- *Quiet Operation* – most are very quiet and you can sneak a photo anytime without anyone hearing you…

- *Auto Mode* – the quality of images produced in point and shoots varies greatly, but in general they shoot very well in auto mode!

- *Price* – in general, point and shoot digital cameras are a very inexpensive. Of course, you can go to the top of the range and spend as much as you would on a cheaper DSLR, but most are in a much more affordable price bracket.
- *LCD Framing* – as I mentioned above, many digital camera users prefer to frame their shots using LCDs. Point and Shoots always come with this ability and some even come with 'flip out' screens that enable their users to take shots from different angles and still see what they're shooting.

Point and Shoot Digital Camera Weaknesses:

- *Image Quality* – point and shoots generally have small image sensors which means that the quality that they produce is generally lower. This is slowly changing in some point and shoots, but in comparison to DSLRs they still have a way to go. It's worth saying, however…that if you're not planning on using your images for major enlargements or in professional applications, that the quality of point and shoot cameras can be more than enough for the average user. Manufacturers are making improvements all the time in their technology and even in the last year or two I've noticed significant image quality improvements.
- *Smaller ISO range* – once again, this is changing slowly (my point and shoot has the ability to shoot to 1600 ISO) but in general, ISO ranges are more limited in point and shoot cameras – this limits them in different shooting conditions.
- *Speed* – point and shoot digital cameras were always notorious for their slowness, particularly their 'shutter lag' (the time between pressing the shutter and when the image is taken). This is the one key feature that separates a DSLR from a Point and Shoot.
- *Manual Controls Limited* – many point and shoot cameras do have the ability to play with a full array of manual settings and controls (or at least make it difficult to do so). They often come with 'aperture priority' and 'shutter priority' modes which are great – but quite often the manual controls are hidden in menu systems and are not as accessible as on a DSLR (if they are there at all).
- *Less Adaptable* - while they are highly portable point and shoot cameras are generally not very adaptable. What you buy when you first get them is what you are stuck with using for years. Some do have lens adapters to give you wider angles or longer zooms but generally most people don't go for these accessories.

Which Point and Shoot Digital Cameras Do I Recommend?

- Once again, let me point to you that I am a Nikon Fan! I suggest any Point and Shoot in the Nikon Family. Pricing ranges from MSRP: $119.00 for the L24, to $500.00 for the P7100.

Should You Buy a DSLR or a Point and Shoot Digital Camera?

- This is ultimately a question that you need to answer for yourself… My answer is to have both (I'm fortunate to be able to do so). I use: Nikon Coolpix L22 for vacations, travel and parties. Nikon D3100 for a backup camera and general fun shots. Nikon D4 and a D2X for the photography business and professional photography. I also have an older retired D1X and D100 in my camera archive collection, along with an old school Pentax K1000 and Minolta Film Cameras that photographed the dinosaurs back in the day.
- If you want a portable camera that takes good pictures that you'll mainly use for small prints, Facebook and emailing…where you will mainly shoot in auto mode, you would probably be very happy with a point and shoot camera :)

Starting a Photography Business

In this article I am going to break down all the overwhelming amount of business information and give you the exact initial steps required to make an official and legal business, specifically, how to start a photography business and get your photography business up and running quickly and working for you!

Step 1 – Write a Business Plan:

- Although there are no legal requirements to having a business plan, it is a valuable document and that will help guide you and get your photography business started on the right track ultimately leading you to success. Putting together a business plan is no easy task, but running a successful business isn't easy either. A well thought out and comprehensive plan should include these topics:
- Description of Business – What type of photography business are you going to be? Large studio or small boutique? Are you going to focus on weddings or family?
- Market Analysis – What is your target market? Who is your ideal customer? What is the competition like in your market? What is the market price point/price range for what you intend on competing against?
- Competitive Advantage – How are you going to be different to gain business over the competitors?
- Operations – Who is going to run the business? What roles will be involved for day to day operation? Is the business scale-able?
- Financing – Is there a need to raise capital/money to get started? If so, how much is needed? How will you get it/who will provide it?
- Goals & Objectives – What do you want to achieve with the business? Write your goals down so you can track to them. Set goals that are of challenge but yet still realistically attainable and set metrics to track your progress.

Step 2 – Choosing a Business Structure:

The first true step and one of the biggest decisions you'll have to make is what type of business entity do you want to operate as. There are significant differences amongst each type so it is important to research and learn about which is best for you as the form of business structure you choose has direct implications on how much paperwork is required, how much or little personal liability is tied to the business and lastly the amount and type of taxes you will have to pay. If you are unsure which is right for you, consulting with a CPA can be a good move to make sure you are making the best choice.

Sole Proprietorship - A sole proprietorship is setup as a single business owner. Profits are taxed at the sole proprietor's individual tax rates, unlike corporations with other tax obligations and schedules.
Pros: Easiest to setup, run and operate
Cons: Owners are personally liable if lawsuit. Personal assets such as houses, cars, etc… can be lost in lawsuit against business.

Partnership – Two or more persons as business owners. Partnerships (the business itself) are not separately taxed, so all profits and losses flow directly to its partners. Either a written or oral agreement must be in place for a partnership outlining the partners and their respective ownership/share of the company.
Pros: Similar to Sole Prop, easy to set up & get going. Pass-thru taxation, file taxes on individual tax returns.
Cons: No liability protection, personal assets at risk.

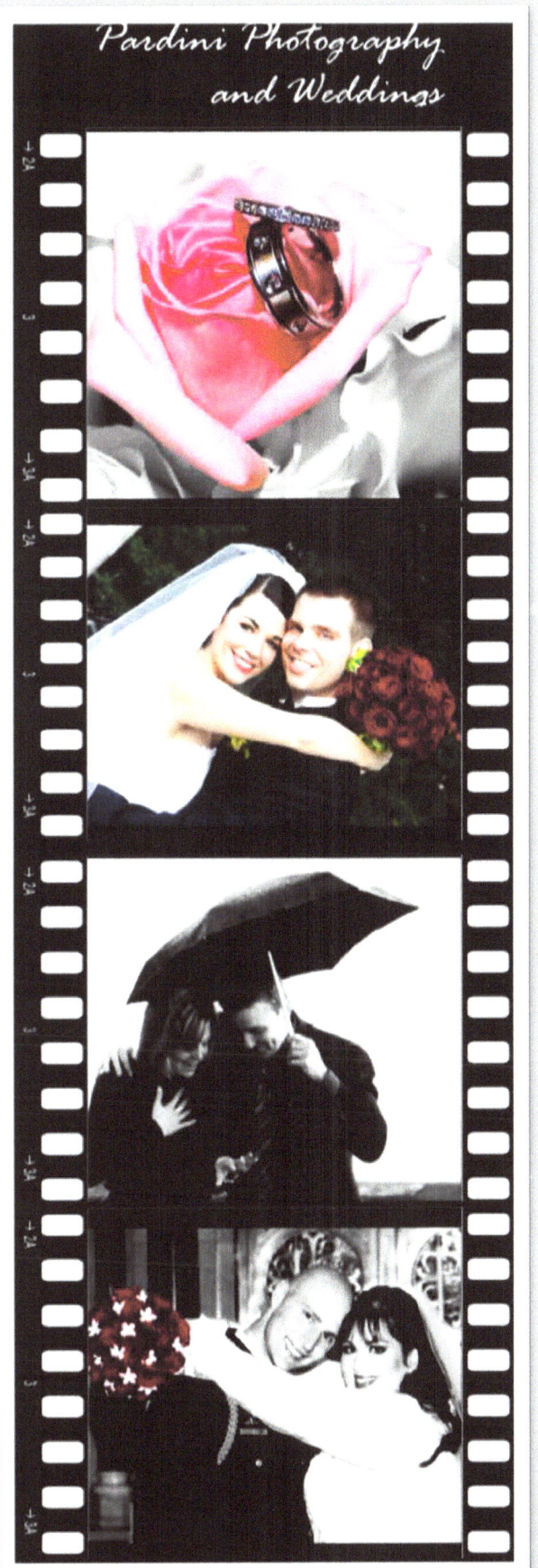

Pardini Photography and Weddings

Corporation - "A corporation is a separate, legal business entity owned by shareholders who enjoy protection from personal liability." Corporations are taxed as a corporation rather than a single person or individual partners.

Pros: Prestige, personal liability protection, can reduce taxes
Cons: Costlier to maintain & setup, more paperwork, can increase taxes

Limited Liability Company - An LLC can be set up for tax purposes to act and operate as a partnership or a corporation. Most often, LLCs are set up to function like a partnership with multiple owners/partners because unlike a general partnership where there is no protection from personal liability, an LLC business structure offers each of the partner's limited liability.

Pros: Liability coverage (like corporation), taxed similar to sole prop or partnership (individual tax returns).
Cons: More formality fees & expenses than sole prop.

So which business structure should you choose? That differs from person to person based on numerous factors and you should do ample research before making a final decision but let the above summary help guide you in your decision making process.

Step 3 – Creating & Registering a Business Name:

You have the business plan in place, you've done your research and know which type of business entity you are going to choose, next up – what are you going to be named?! If you aren't feeling creative at all and would prefer to go the "personal name" route for your photography business than you are all set and ready to register your name; but if you would prefer to come up with a unique name here are some of my tips on "what" makes a good business name.

Easy to pronounce & spell

Easy to remember

Likeability/Uniqueness

Not too long

Availability (no one else has the name and/or available for web domain address)

Once you have picked out the perfect name for your photography business and you have already researched to know the name is available, you are ready to make it official. If you are choosing to use a business name that doesn't include your own name i.e.

"Pardini Photography and Weddings ", you will have to register a "fictitious business name statement" also known as: "Doing Business As" or "DBA" with the county clerk of where you plan to operate at. Please note that the actual person and place where you file your DBA and register your name is completely dependent on where you are located and therefore different for everyone. In addition, the fees in doing so will vary from county to county too. Please note, not all states require the registering of fictitious business names or DBAs.

Step 4 – Paying Taxes:

Depending on where you are located and doing business you may have different taxes that are applicable to you. The type of business structure you choose as shown above in step 2 will dictate what type of taxes and what tax schedules are applicable and needed. In addition to federal & state income taxes you may be liable to pay sales & use tax, payroll tax (if you have employees) or other special taxes or fees applicable to your county or state. It is important to find out all the taxes applicable to your business based on business type and also location. If you have to register a fictitious business name with the county where you operate make sure to discuss them about your tax obligations as they will be a key resource for you.

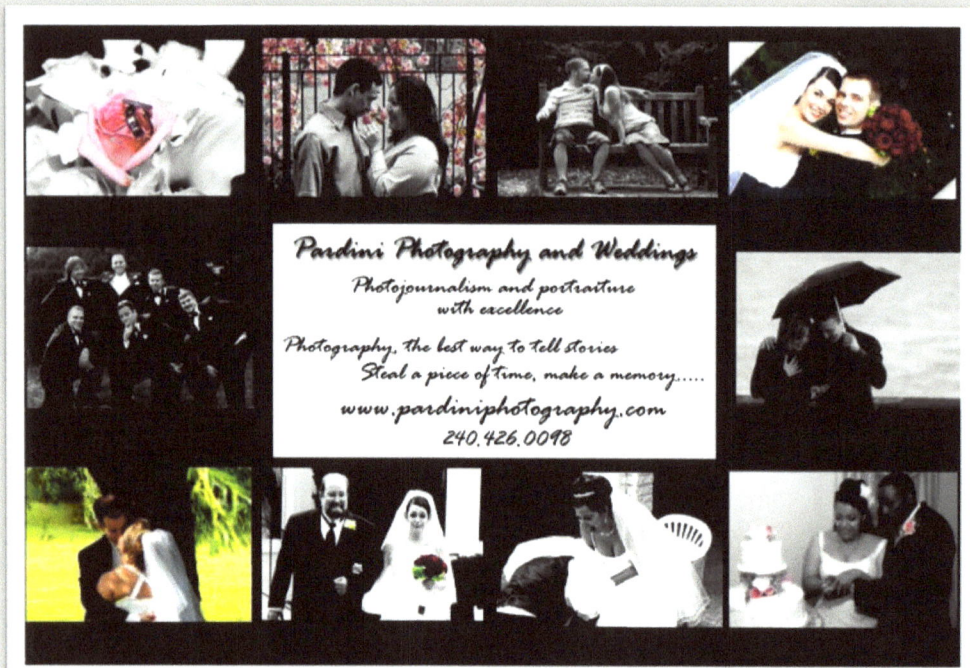

Once you have all of the above steps taken care of you are an official business and ready to get out there and start booking some business!

Invest in the Right Equipment:

While a bad workman may blame his tools, a good photographer knows that the right quality equipment can make a big difference to his results. This will be your principal investment and it pays dividends to buy the best you can afford. Do your research and work out how best to allocate your budget to get the most useful equipment. When you are starting out, it may be worth taking out a loan or seeking third-party investment.

Think about which camera and lenses will be most appropriate for your chosen area of specialization and then select a computer and photo editing software. You will also need to decide whether you are going to rent a studio and what sort of lighting you will require.

Building a Portfolio Builds Credibility:

To charge a professional fee for your photography, you will need to convince potential clients that you have the skill and experience to deliver the job. It's vital that you have a professional looking portfolio, weighted towards your area of specialization.

Professional presentation of your work is critical and if you are not prepared to throw good money at it, you will not stand out in the 'theatre of presentation' to your clients. You could expect to pay anything from $150 to $1,000.

If you expect people to pay top dollar, you need to be able to show them they will receive high quality results. It took us years to build our photography portfolio and it's still a work in progress. Building, editing and refining photography portfolios is an ongoing process throughout your entire working life as a photographer.

Since you are just starting out I recommend that you take on some pro-bono jobs to build your portfolio and resume. Or see if you can assist another photographer at no cost but ask for copy right use of the photographs you take for your portfolio.

Online Marketing:

As well as being an expert photographer, you'll need to learn all about search engine optimization (SEO) and social networking to promote your services. If you find it hard to do it all yourself, then investing in a monthly contract with a reputable SEO agency will definitely be worth your while. We were very lucky to get to the first pages of Google for a large number of keywords in a little over a year and pretty much stay there building on the quality of work we produce.

Professional photography is a highly competitive industry. Your chances of success will be multiplied if you know your craft and if you take the time to gain experience working for someone else. However, once you know the ropes, running your own photographic business is a challenge that will bring its own rewards.

Basic Startup Costs:

Make a list of what you need, prioritize it and slowly start purchasing items and checking things off. Running a photography business is not cheap, so make sure you're pricing helps cover this:

- Website Hosting: free - $75 + /annual Design: Free to $10,000 +
- Online marketing: $400 + /annual
- Business cards: $35.00 +
- Portfolio: $150.00 + (suggest a few photo books, computer or iPad slideshow and print album
- Camera equipment: $600 +
- Backup camera equipment: $600 + (since this is a business a backup or triple backup is a good idea)
- Editing software: Photoshop Elements $70.00 or Photoshop CS versions $1,000.00

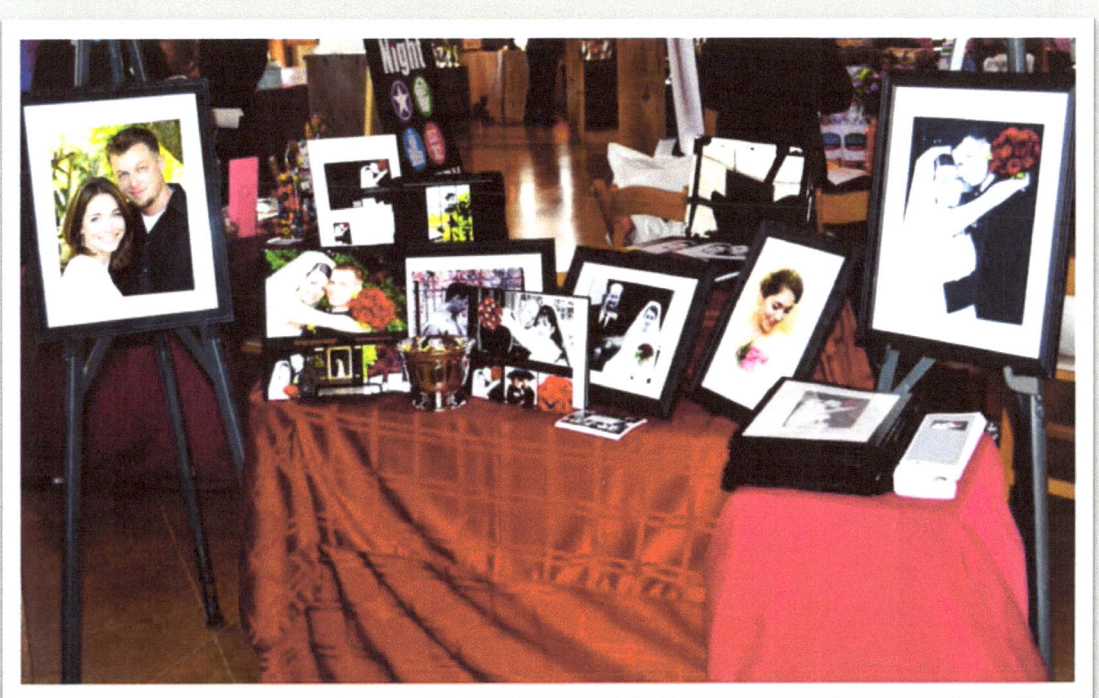

Task	Duration
Learning and studding photography	Lifetime
Book store (build your book arsenal)	1 day
Find a mentor wedding photographer	1 week
Work alongside wedding/portrait photographer	1-5 times
Develop business name	3 weeks
Make your sample album (portfolio)	3 weeks
Plan your website	1 week
Surf the web and lookup other businesses like yours in your area and see what they are doing right and wrong	3 weeks
Decide on pricing and packages	3 days
Design or higher a web designer for your site	1 month
Develop business plan	3 weeks
Purchase and learn accounting software	3 weeks
Create business forms	3 weeks
Design and have business cards printed	3 weeks
Obtain EIN with IRS	1 month
Register your business name	3 weeks
Apply for LLC, INC, etc.	1 month
Setup business checking account	1 day
Determine breakeven margins	2 weeks
Create sales projections	2 weeks
Devolve annual budget	3 weeks
Ensure current equipment is suitable or purchase or rent new equipment	1 week
Develop a marketing plan	2 weeks
Develop branding: colors, logo, etc	3 weeks
Advertise on 3 wedding vendor websites	1 month
Grand opening	1 day
Review business at 6 months, 12 months, 18 months and 24 months	1 week

Pardini Photography and Weddings

Check out our new book on Amazon! The book gives advanced tips to help make your wedding day as picturesque as possible and to give you helpful posing techniques.
This book is a free gift to anyone that books a wedding with us.

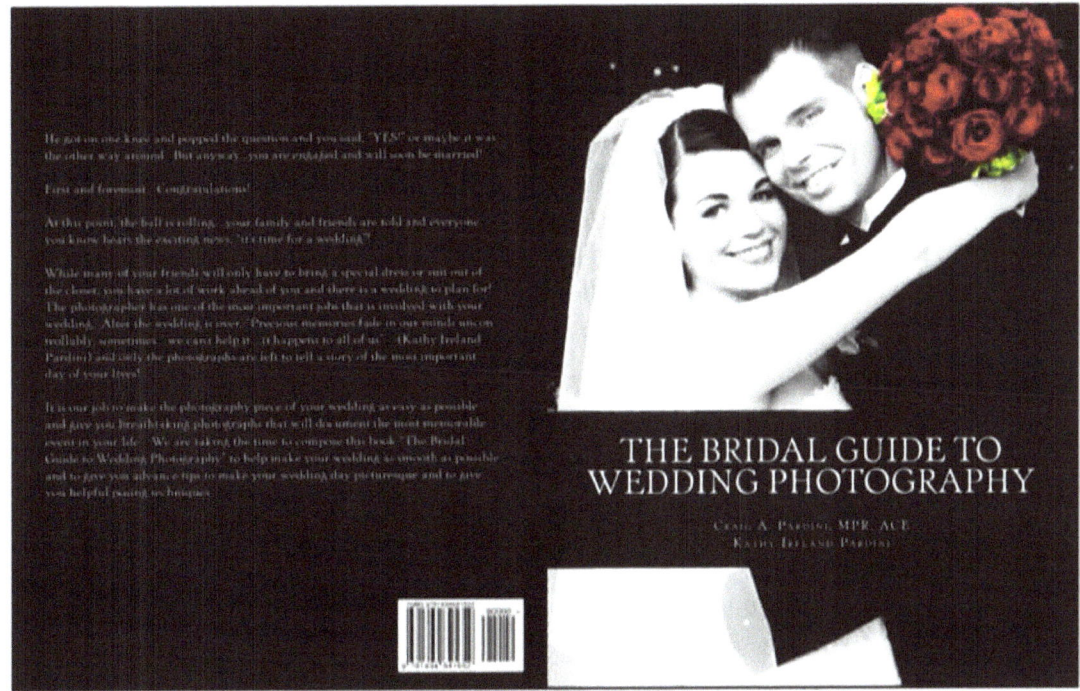

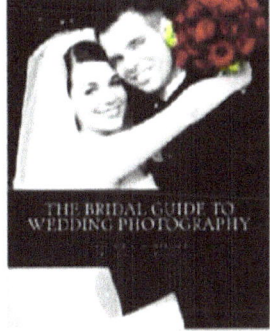

The Bridal Guide to Wedding Photography Paperback – December 31, 2013
by Craig A Pardini (Author), Kathy Ireland Pardini (Author)

Be the first to review this item

Paperback
$15.40

He got on one knee and popped the question and you said "YES!" or maybe it was the other way around. But anyway, you are engaged and will soon be married! First and foremost, Congratulations! At this point, the ball is rolling, your family and friends are told and everyone you know hears the exciting news, "it's time for a wedding"! While many of your friends will only have to bring a special dress or suit out of the closet, you have a lot of work ahead of you and there is a wedding to plan for! The photographer has one of the most important jobs that is involved with your wedding. After the wedding is over, "Precious memories fade in our minds uncontrollably, sometimes, we can't help it, it happens to all of us" - (Kathy Ireland-Pardini) and only the photographs are left to tell a story of the most important day of your life! It is our job to make the photography piece of your wedding as easy as possible and give you breathtaking photographs that will document the most memorable event in your life. We are taking the time to compose this book "The Bridal Guide to Wedding Photography" to help make your wedding as smooth as possible and to give you advance tips to make your wedding day picturesque and to give you helpful posing techniques

▸ Read less

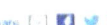
+ Add to Collection

Share [...]

Taking Photos from an Airplane

This article talks about two of my passions….photography and flying! If you love photography, than it is obvious that you are interested in things that are visually interesting. When you are on your next airplane ride, I strongly suggest that you ask for a window seat!   The view you see can be spectacular, and by following the few tips below, you can take some very intriguing photographs!

There are some challenges when taking pictures from an airplane.   First, you need a pretty clean and clear window. Next you run into the reflection issue. If the sun is shining in the window, you will see your reflection. You will need to get your lens as close to the window as possible. This will help eliminate, or at least reduce, reflections!

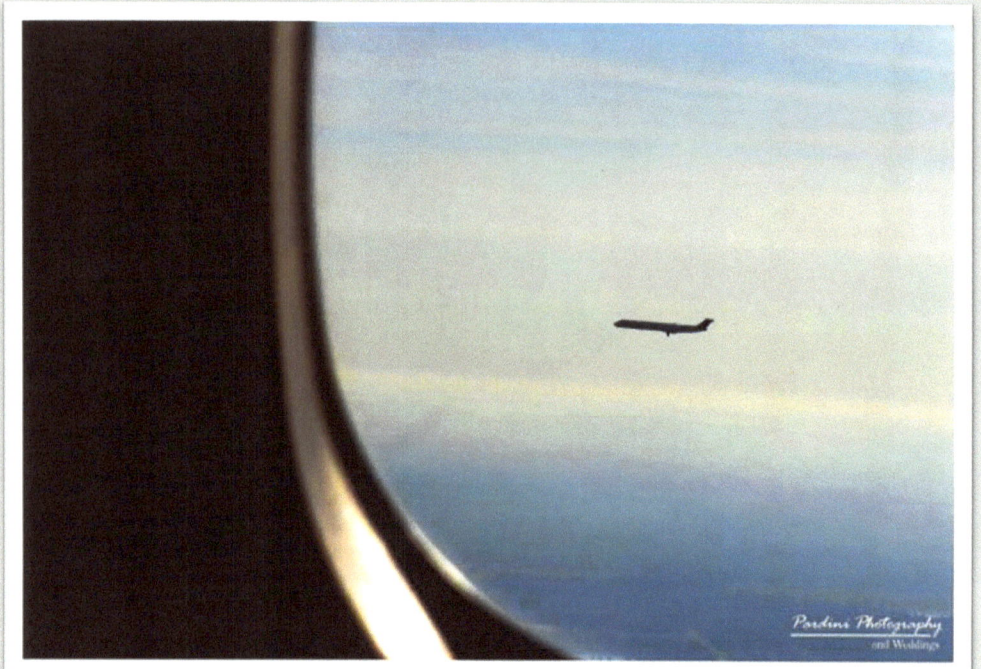

There are a few things to be aware of when you take your aviation photographs. First, if you are using a DSLR, I suggest that you have an ISO setting of 400 and not use flash. Since you are moving at 500+ miles per hour, you will also need to go with shutter speed priority. If you need to use flash, put your lenses close to the window as possible.   If you're not close to the window, the flash may fire lighting up the entire frame—probably not the effect you were looking for.

It's also possible that the camera will try to focus on the window Plexiglas rather than the view in the distance. If that happens, you can do a few different tricks: Most point and shoot cameras will let you set the focus to infinity (often indicated by a mountain icon). Or if you are using a DSLR, switch to manual focus and use your focusing ring on the barrel of the lenses.

After you made the correct settings, you can start having fun. Look for lines and patterns in the landscape below….especially if you are traveling over the mid-west states like Colorado and Wyoming.   Other airplanes

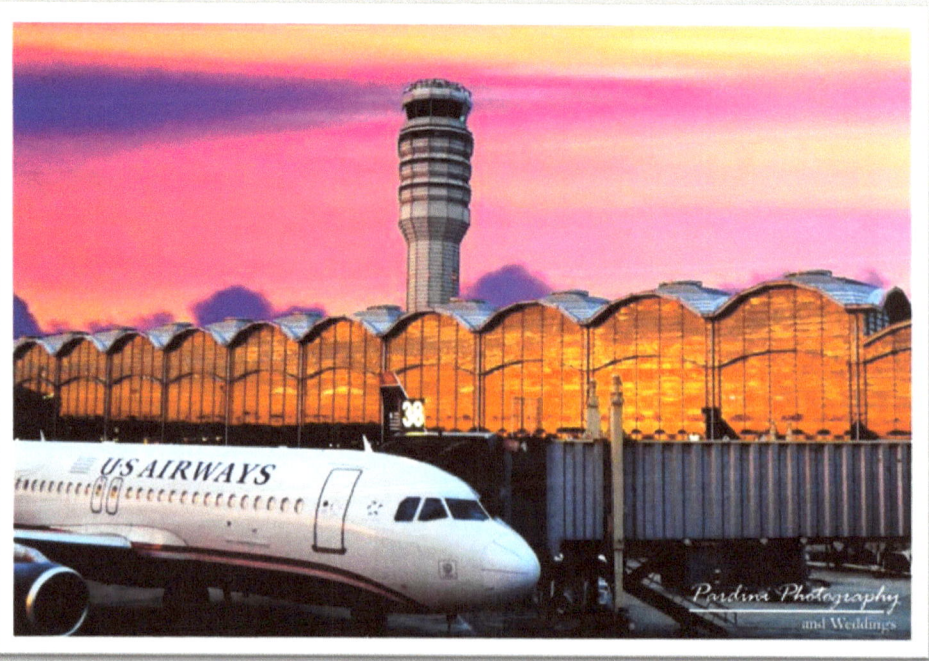

on the tarmac.   Other airplanes taking off. If flying over mountain terrain, look for patches of snow.   Zoom in and out for different composition style shots! Sometimes capturing the planes winglets can make a nice shot as well! What is really cool is capturing the contrails (A trail of condensed water from an aircraft at high altitude, seen as a white streak against the sky).

When flying at high altitudes, it is normal to lose some contrast. That can be altered when editing your photos later! You will be amazed what a difference a photograph can make by adding brightness and contrast when editing!

The window seat can be a great way to fly, especially if you like to take pictures. Plus, you'll never get bumped by the flight attendant or asked to get up when the person flying next to you needs to use the lavatory. Also, if you are afraid of flying, this will help keep you at ease, since your concentration will be on the photos and not soaring through the sky at 500 miles per hour in a steel tube! Since I am also an aviation nut, I have to mentioned, when you feel turbulence, it is the same as driving over a speed-bump to the pilots :)

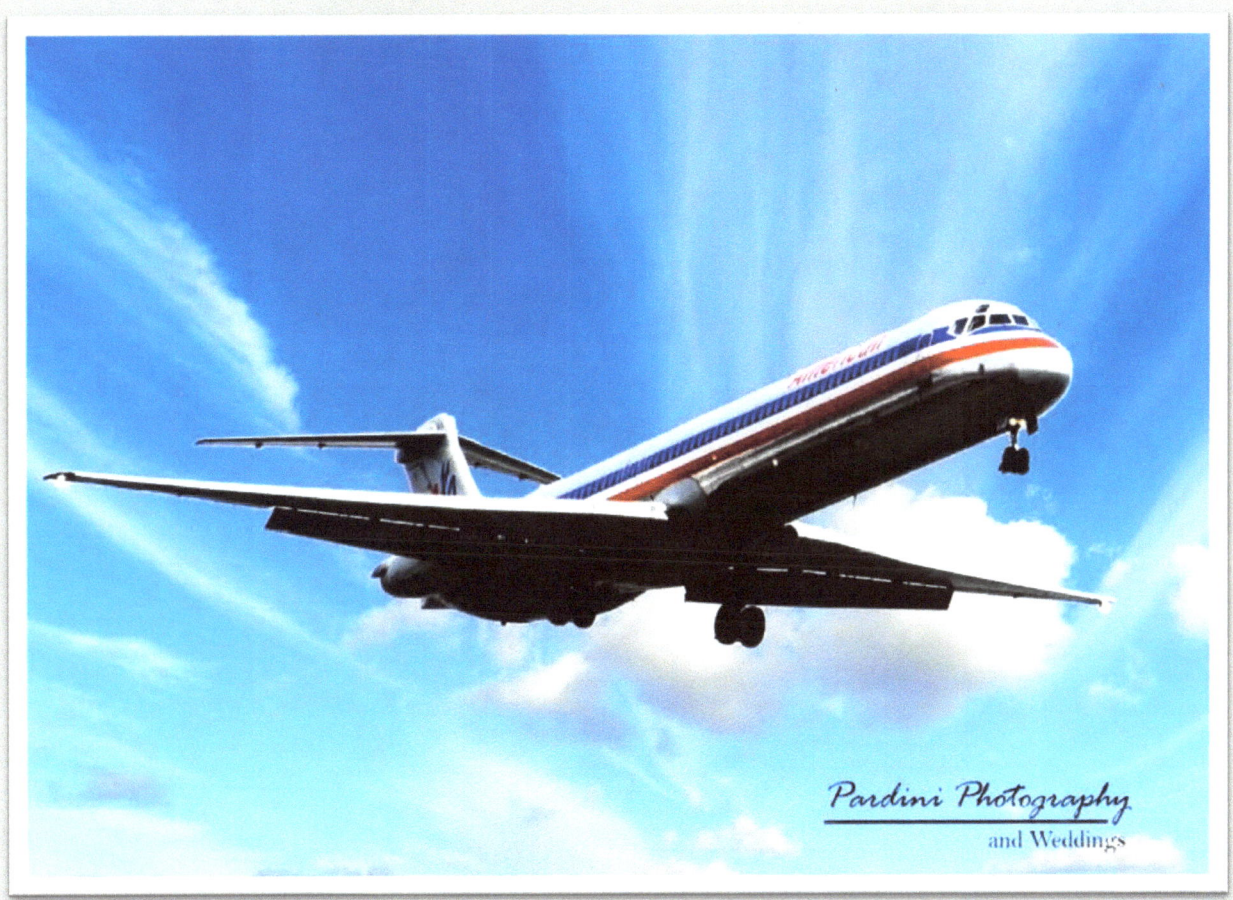

Thanksgiving / Food Photography

As you may have noticed, taking great food photographs is quite difficult. I love the holiday time...not only for the festivities and great food, but a great time to take photographs and experimenting with composition. Below is just the tip of the iceberg of ideas that can help you take better Thanksgiving / Food photographs. Hope this helps and I wish you a very Happy Thanksgiving!

Make a List:

First and foremost, it's a great idea to write down a list of the photos you'd like to capture. In the hustle and bustle of the holiday activities, there's a good chance you'll simply forget to take some pictures until it's too late. Take the food, for example: You probably want to shoot the turkey and the pies before they're cut into. Make a list of the important scenes. I like to shoot the fully dressed table, laid out with the turkey and fixings, before the guests invade. I also like

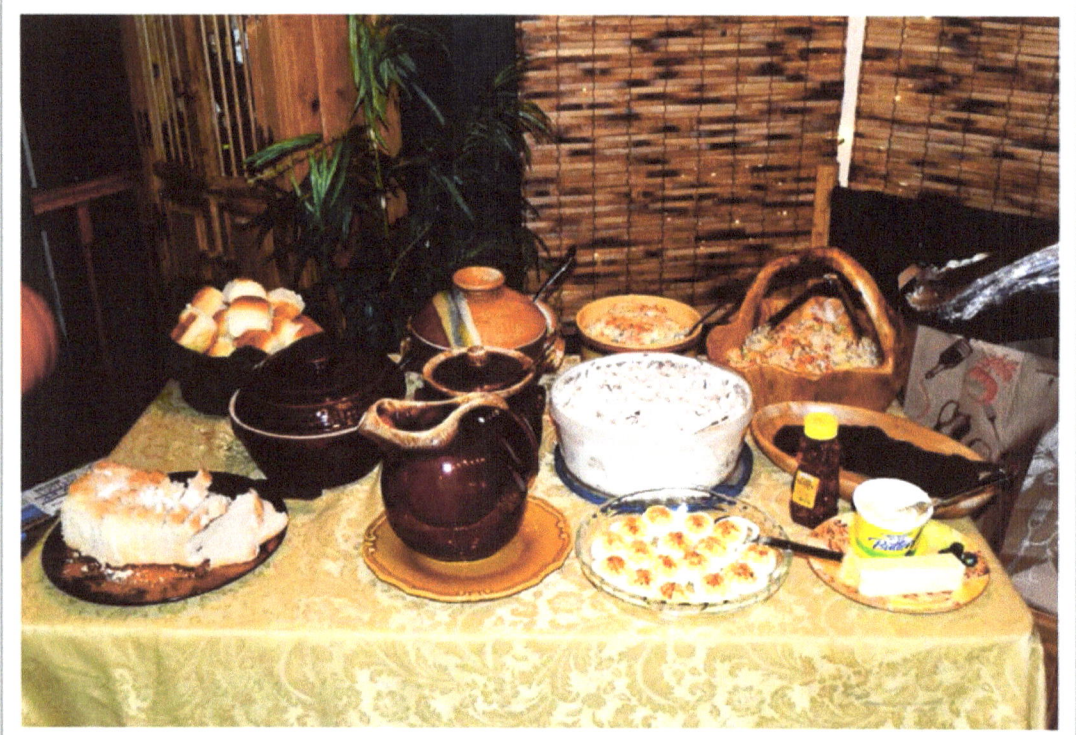

to get a few different perspectives of the other side dishes, such as from directly overhead and from the side. A dish looks more pleasing to the eyes if shot at an angle vs. straight down on it or directly from the front.

Work the Lighting:

I know that you're busy entertaining guests, making the big meal, and keeping the family dog from stealing sweet potatoes off the kitchen counter :) But amidst all that, you should also remember to optimize the lighting for your photos. As I've said many times before, the camera's flash is really a last resort...your camera will give much better results with ambient light. Turn on as many lights as possible and crank up your ISO setting. This control, which affects how sensitive the camera is to light is usually best left in its lowest position. But rather than use the flash, it's better to increase the camera's ISO to 800 or even higher so that you can take better advantage of the naturally available light.

Use HDR Mode Instead of a Flash:

If your camera has a built-in high dynamic range mode, use it instead of the flash. Some cameras (especially camera phones like some iPhone and Windows Phone models) have an HDR mode that optimizes for light and dark areas to give you a better overall exposure without resorting to the flash. Even better, these built-in HDR modes tweak the exposure of a single photo instead of taking a series of shots and combining them, so the whole process is fairly fast (about the same as taking a normal shot).

Shoot From Above:

You might be inclined to take the traditional dinner table family portrait from eye level, but that means you've got all sorts of clutter…including candles, glasses, and perhaps even the turkey itself…getting in the way. A better solution is to get above eye level and shoot down towards your subjects. Not only does this get you above the fray, but photos from a higher elevation are often more flattering to the people you're photographing. You can do that by setting the camera on a tripod, or you can stand on a chair or stairs.

Get Creative With Depth Of Field:

Not all of your subject has to be in focus as slowly blurring part of it can add interest to the shot as well as draw the eye to one particular part of the frame. It works well with lines of produce or where you have lots of the same produce in your shot. You still need enough of the produce to be in focus so it looks like you did it purposely rather than your viewer thinking you just took a bad shot so experiment with different apertures until you find something that works.

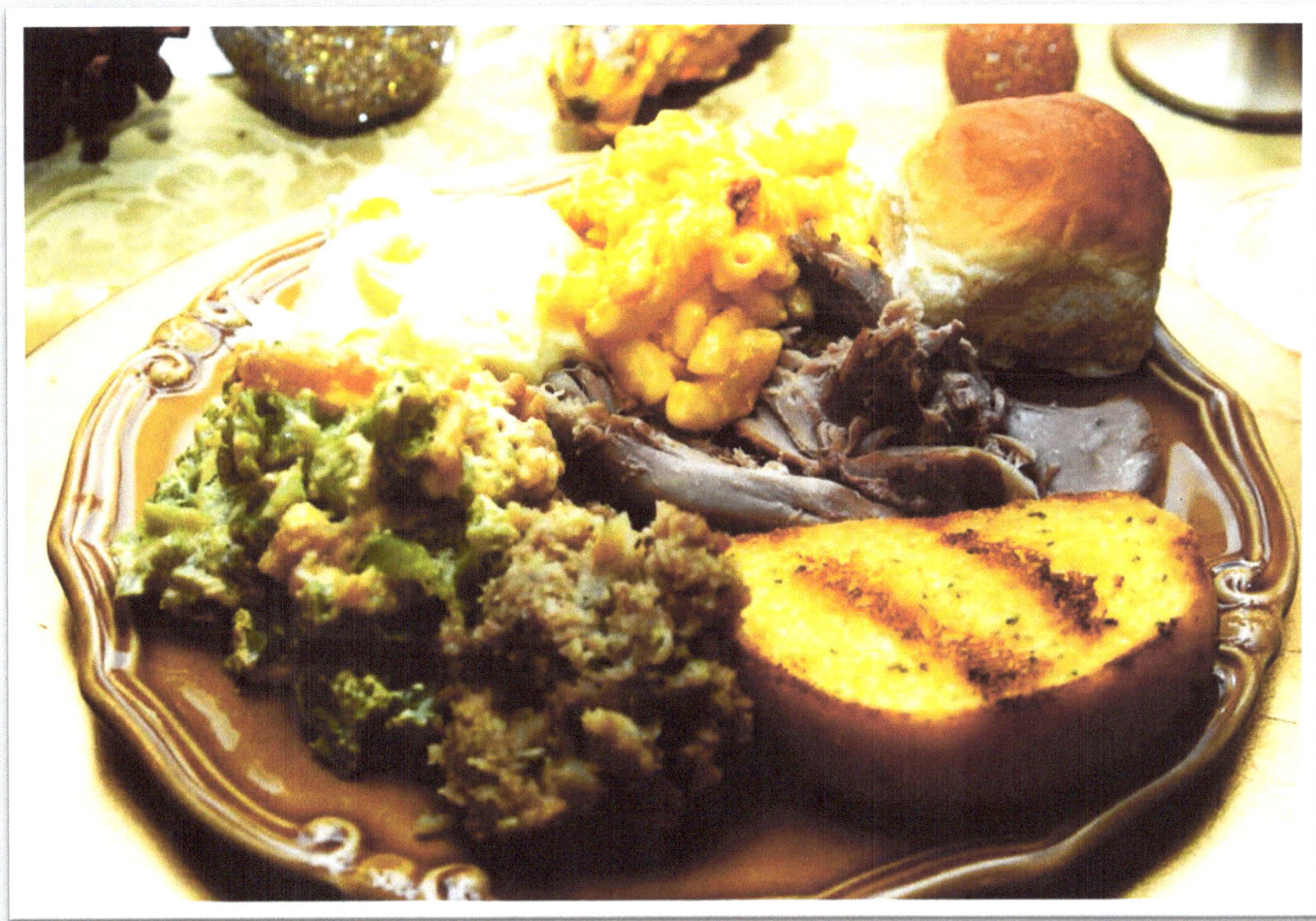

The Bouquet Toss

Here is an example of what can go wrong and what you can do to avoid this mishap.

Problem: Bride throws her bouquet up and hits a light fixture or the ceiling and it fall to the ground where a bridesmaid has to pick it up.

Solution: Ask your photographer to chat with you beforehand and pick an area with high clearance with no obstructions in the background. Toss behind and out.

It is good to take it slow and tease the crowd by looking behind you a few times before throwing the bouquet. This builds excitement and also give the photographer a couple of opportunities for some nice shots of the bride with her female guests waiting in anticipation.   It is best for the photographer to take the photo from the side or in front of the bride...

Bonus Tip for Grooms: You know that garter you want to hurl like a fast ball in the world series? It is as light as a feather. It's not going to go far. Stay fairly close to the guys and give a light toss to keep it airborne for a little while.

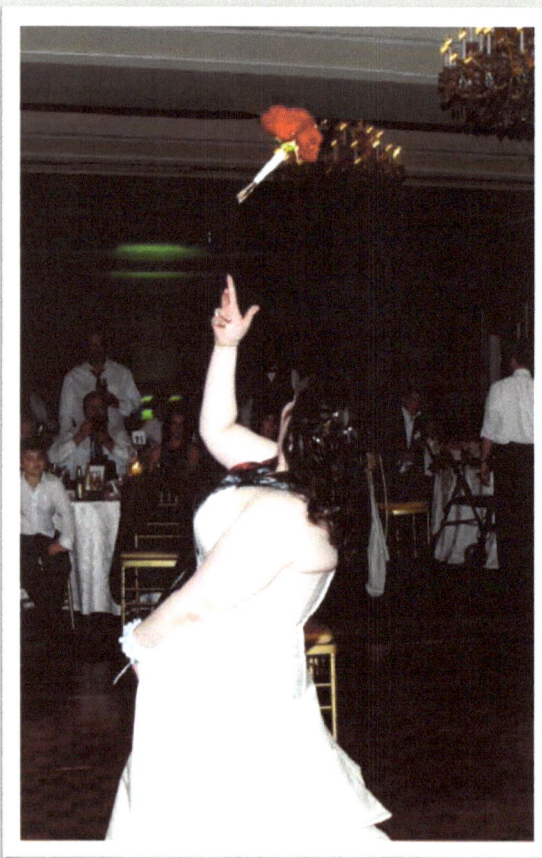 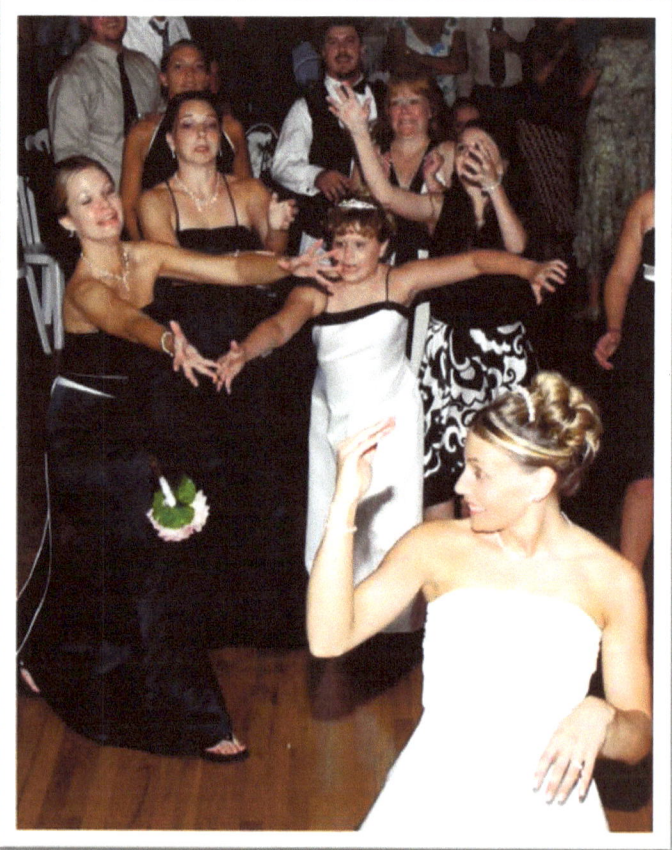

Understanding ISO Settings

Photography, the art of painting with light is made possible of three different light exposures: shutter speed, aperture and ISO (also known as film speed). Shutter and aperture are controls for adjusting how much light comes into the camera. How much light that is needed is determined by the ISO settings or film speed.

The normal ISO range is between 200 - 1600. With some digital cameras you can go extremely low: 50 or as high as 102,400 marked as H1, H2, etc.

The brighter the light, the lower the ISO setting needs to be. An ISO setting of 200 is often used in bright situations or sunny outdoor days. If you do not have a lot of light, or need a fast shutter speed, you will need to increase the ISO setting.

Each time you double the ISO setting, E.G., going from 200 to 400, the camera needs only half as much light for the same exposure. For example, if you had a shutter speed of 1/250 at 200 ISO, switching to 400 ISO would let you get the same exposure at 1/500 second if in the same light. This is why high ISOs are so often used indoors, especially at

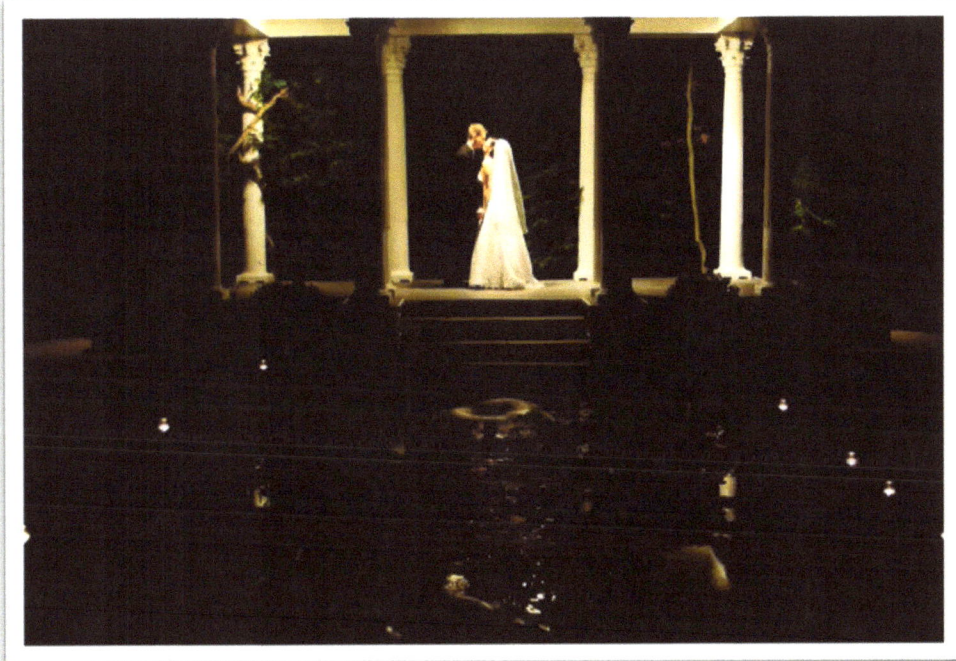

sporting events. If you need a fast shutter speed, it is suggested that you choose an ISO setting of 1600 or above.

Keep in mind that the higher the ISO, the more noise you will have in your photograph. Photo noise was called grain back in the film days... The higher the ISO setting gives you a matching decrease in quality. With today's digital cameras you can shoot a clear image at an ISO setting of 1600. Larger pixel cameras and pro DSLR cameras with large sensors will help reduce the amount of noise!

That is one of the reasons why DSLR cameras perform better than the smaller point and shoot cameras in low light. Some high-end cameras have built in noise reduction settings. If you are using RAW mode, you also have a good chance or reducing additional noise when editing.

ISO comes down to a catch 22. You want to keep a low ISO for high quality images with low noise, but need a faster shutter speed for a sharp no blur photographs! By knowing your camera ISO setting can help you make good decisions that will give you clear, sharp and professional photographs! I suggest that you practice and learn the proper settings.

Understanding Aperture

If You Have Ever Wondered What the Camera Aperture Is...

Aperture refers to the opening of a lens's diaphragm that light passes through to make an image (see image). It is calibrated in f/stops and is generally numbered: 1.4, 2, 2.8, 4, 5.6, 8, 11 and 16. The lower the f/stop, the more exposure it has because the diaphragm is winder. However, the wider the diagram, the lower depth of field you will have in your photographs. This may seem a little strange at first, but will become clearer as you take pictures at varying f/stops. I suggest that you read your camera's manual first to learn how to set your camera for Aperture Priority, and then try experimenting to get comfortable with changing the aperture and recognizing the effects different apertures will have on your images...

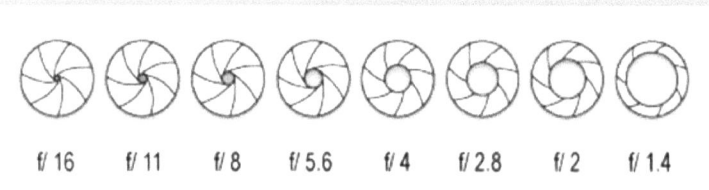

f/ 16   f/ 11   f/8   f/ 5.6   f/ 4   f/ 2.8   f/ 2   f/ 1.4

How Aperture Affects Depth of Field in Your Photographs...

Depth of field is defined as 'the zone of acceptable sharpness in front of and behind the subject on which the lens is focused.' In layman's terms, it is how sharp or blurry is the area behind your subject.

Here's the Equation In All of This...

The lower the f/stop, the larger the opening there is in the lens, the less depth of field, the blurrier the background will be. The higher the f/stop, the smaller the opening in the lens, the greater the depth of field, the sharper the background will be. Tip – if you want your subject to be in focus, but don't like the background, shoot with a lower f/stop!

How Aperture Affects Shutter Speed...

The f/stop also affects shutter speed. Using a low f/stop means more light is entering the lens and the shutter does not need to stay open as long for a good exposure. This means faster shutter speed. Again, the reverse is also true: using a high f/stop means less light will enter the lens causing the shutter staying open a little longer which translates into a slower shutter speed and a good chance for a blurry photograph.

How Do You Change the Aperture You Ask???

All lenses have a maximum aperture, and all NIKKOR lenses list the widest possible aperture on the lens barrel. Some zoom lenses will detail something like f/3.5-5.6 on the lens barrel or 1:3.5-5.6. These numbers, the 3.5 and the 5.6, are referring to the maximum aperture or widest opening the lens can achieve for each end of the zoom range. Some higher end lenses can maintain the largest aperture throughout the entire zoom range, so only one number is detailed.

For portraits or classical style photography, I suggest choosing a large aperture (lower f/stop, like f2.8) so you can create a very shallow depth of field with only the subject, or just a portion of the subject, in focus. This helps direct the viewer's attention to the subject.

For landscape style photography where you can see as much detail as possible from foreground to background; you will want to achieve the maximum depth. You will do this by of field by choosing a small aperture (higher f/stop, like f/8 or f/11).

Always thought it is funny and contradicting that a 'large aperture is a low f/stop' and a 'small aperture is a high f/stop' It is just the same as to the question: why do you drive on the parkway and park on the driveway?...

What Goes Into Wedding Photography

There are several unseen areas that the photographers do for your wedding day photography. A lot of this is overlooked by the clients and also is factored into the overall package cost. This will hopefully shed some light on what you are paying for besides the actually finished product and picture taking…

Below are some bullet points that capture what a wedding photographer may do for you. Not all photographers may do this…I can only go off of what we, at Pardini Photography and Weddings do, so you have the best day possible and the photographs are picture perfect!

It is not as easy as some may think… this just covers what we do in dealing with the clients and not the business part of things, such as: bookkeeping, marketing, and website maintenance, tax prep, etc., etc.

Getting To Know You (2 hours):

- Respond to initial inquire (phone call or email): 5-10 minutes
- Emails or phone calls prior to consultation meeting: 10-15 minutes
- Consultation meeting: 1.5 hours
- Follow-up emails after consultation meeting: 5-10 minutes

Engagement Photography Session (15 hours):

- Engagement photography session: 2 hours
- Uploading photographs to computer and making redounded backups: 30 minutes
- Editing engagement photographs: 8 hours (2 hours per day for 4 days)
- Post editing photographs: renumbering, burning to disk and making picturesque disk labels and covers: 1 hour
- Designing webpage to feature photographs in a slideshow: 30 minutes
- Creating the DVD slideshow documentary and burning to disk: 2 hours
- Meeting with the clients to deliver the finished engagement package or mailing out: 1 hour

Wedding Prep (1 hour):

- 1-2 follow-up conference calls with the clients to cover last minute details: 45 minutes
- Pre wedding day: checking all equipment, charging batteries, inventory and packing everything up: 30 minutes

The Wedding (42 hours):

- Arrive at starting destination 1 hour early to prepare and take location photographs: 1 hour
- Wedding day photographs: 8 hours
- Stay past ending contract time to ensure we capture special ending moments: 1-2 hours
- Uploading photographs to computer and making redounded backups: 30 minutes
- Editing wedding photographs: 24 hours (2 hours per day for 12 days)
- Post editing photographs: renumbering, burning to disk and making picturesque disk labels and covers: 1 hour
- Designing webpage to feature photographs in a slideshow: 30 minutes
- Creating the DVD slideshow documentary and burning to disk: 4 hours

- If prints and albums orders add an additional: 4-6 hours
- Meeting with the clients to deliver the finished engagement package or mailing out: 1 hour

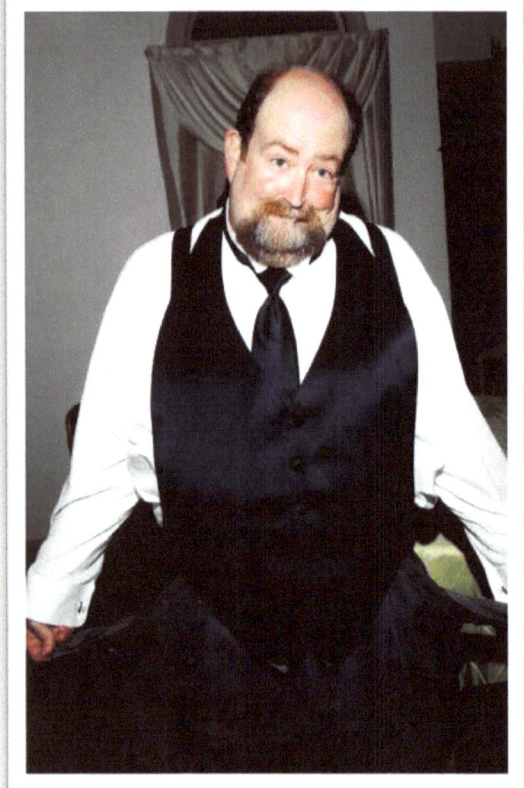

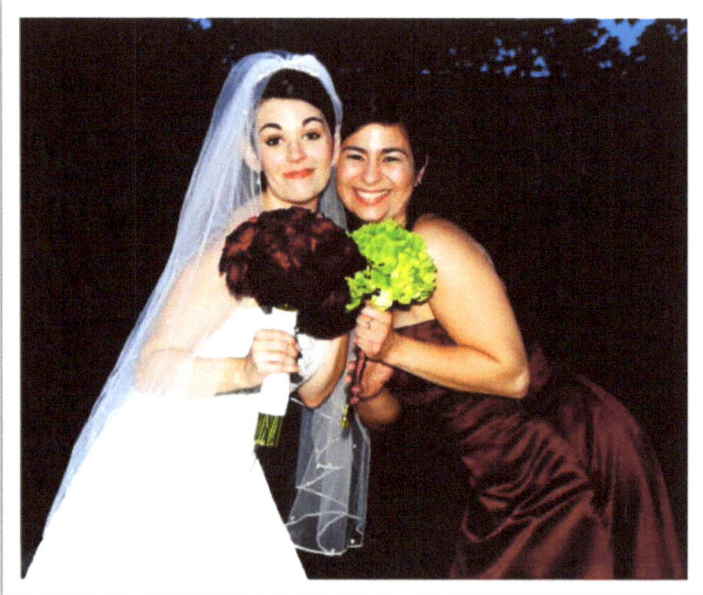

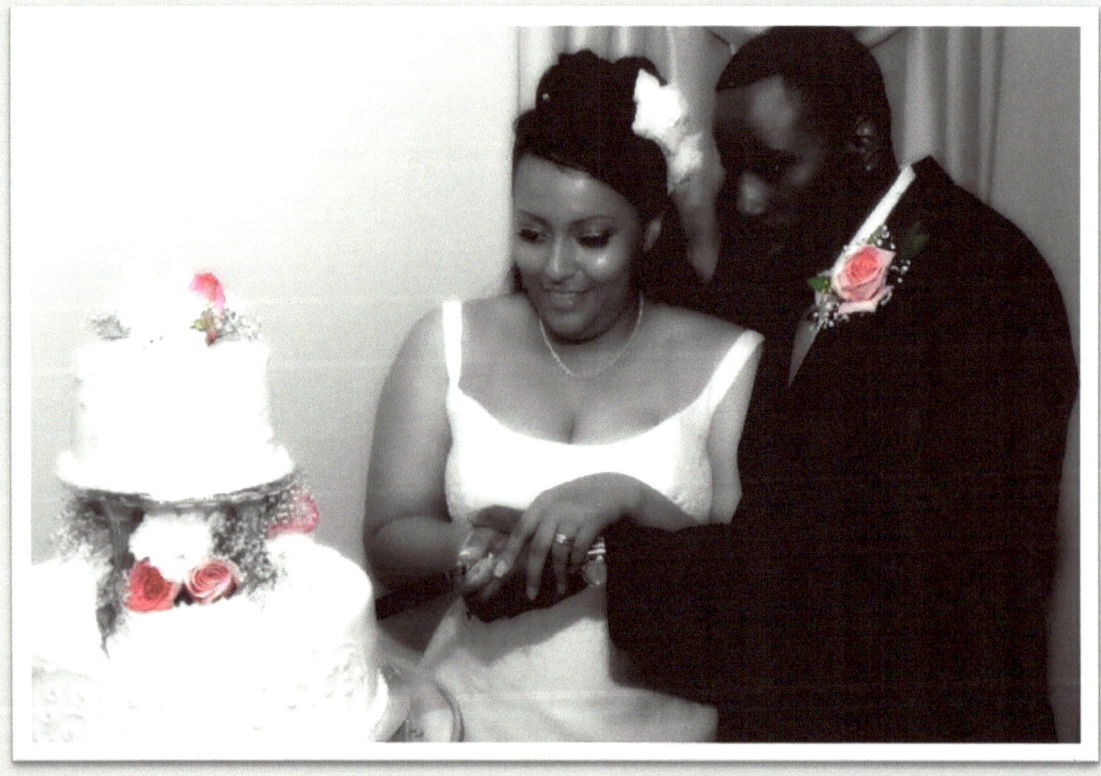

What is Wedding Photojournalism Photography

I have been asked a lot recently what 'Wedding Photojournalism Photography' is… I would like to take a few minutes to answer that question:

Wedding Photojournalism is a popular style of wedding photography today. Couples who choose photojournalists to capture their wedding day feel the traditional photography style is old and looking for something new and different.

Photojournalism is a skill, not just the name of a style of photography. A wedding photojournalist is a photographer who is talented in capturing the moments as they occur throughout the day. Photojournalists capture images that tell a story from start to finish in photographs.

Wedding photojournalist usually arrives before the bride starts getting ready and stays until they take last photo of the bride and groom leaving the reception. The photographer unobtrusively captures each moment of the day, this way the photographs are not posed or staged and there are no interruptions of the day! Since the bride, groom, wedding party, family and gusts are unaware the camera is there, events are captured in a genuine state. True emotion is also caught and revealed using this style of photography. A lot of the photographs also look great in black and white showing a truly storybook effect. (When we photograph your day we take 100% color and give you copies of photographs in black and white that are appropriate) The end result is a narrative collection of images that show actual emotions and experiences of the entire day start to finish. This style of photographs also gives you candid and artistic photos and a relaxed way of being photographed.

Not all photographers have this talent, it is something that is natural and a talent you are born with. I can teach almost anyone to use a camera and take decent photographs; however, no one can be taught how to have an impeccable eye and intuition to take a true documentary of your special day!

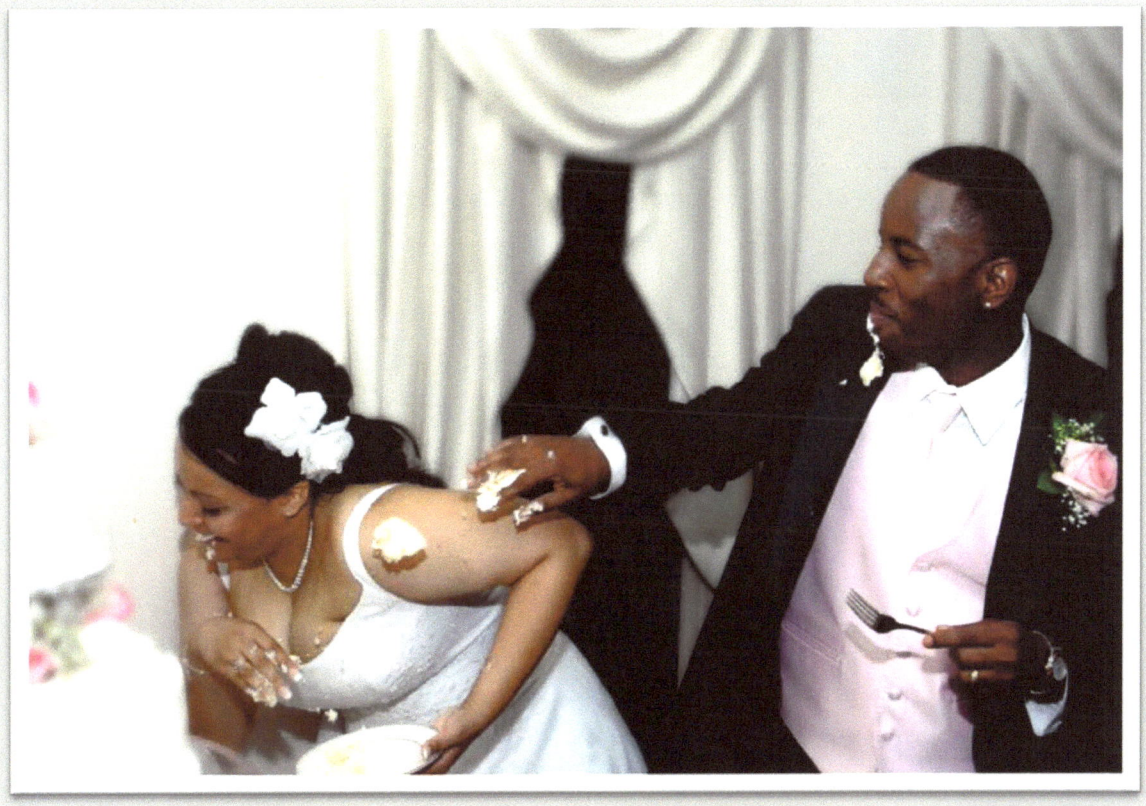

What to Look For When Purchasing a New DSLR Camera

Photographs are memories; and the old saying goes, 'a photo is worth a thousand of words'. Precious memories fade (we can't help it), however, photographs help preserve these memories!

Photography has become an effective means of communicating with loved ones and friends who we may not see as often as we want because of distance or busy schedules… That is why today more and more people are investing in digital cameras. If you are serious about owning a quality camera with a wide array of features and the flexibility to add additional lenses, a digital SLR camera is your best choice!

Before you decide on the camera that will best suit your needs and budget, you have to keep several factors in mind as to what to look for before buying your new digital SLR camera…

What to Look For When Buying a New Digital SLR Camera?

There are many factors to consider in advance so that you will know what type of camera will best fit your needs. First and foremost, how much are you willing to spend for a DSLR camera and what are you using it for?

There is a wide selection of digital SLR cameras available: there are low cost very affordable cameras for people who wish only to take photos for fun and sharing with family and friends. These cameras normally cost around $300.00 - $400.00. There are others that are extremely expensive $5,000 + and are for the professional photographer needing tons of functions and machine gun snapping and focusing. Mid-range cameras cost around $500 - $1500.00. Mid-range cameras work for the serious photographs looking to further the hobby or semi-professional photographers. Majority of photographers will fall somewhere in the middle!

Image resolution or megapixels, is important; however it does not necessarily mean that you need a camera with the highest megapixel count to get the best photos! If you only need pictures that you want to share on on the web, Facebook, email, etc. you probably do not need a DSLR with the highest megapixels, all you need is an average one. However, if you anticipate on making enlargements or cropping a lot of your photos, you will need a camera with high megapixels.

Below is a chart to show you what amount of megapixels are needed for the size prints you may need to maintain a clear photograph.

Clear Maximum Print Size	Megapixels Needed
4 x 6"	2 megapixels
5 x 7"	3 megapixels
8 x 10"	5 megapixels
11 x 14"	6 megapixels
16 x 20"	8 megapixels
20 x 30" Poster	11 megapixels

What is a megapixel you ask? Pictures are created with small pieces of color called pixels. Digital cameras capture images as pixels. Simply put, a megapixel is equal to one million pixels. Digital images are made up of thousands of this tiny, tile like picture elements. The more pixels, the higher the image resolution. Resolution relates primarily to print size and the amount of detail an image has when viewed on a computer monitor. The number of megapixels has little to do with actual camera quality or the quality of a photo it is capable of producing. Factors such as camera sensor and the optical quality of a lens play much more important roles in these areas.

The size of the camera is a consideration to some…. Although, some high end DSLR cameras are bulky. If you want to use a camera when you go on a vacation, a light and handy model such as the Nikon Coolpix or something along those lines may be your best bet! But those are not SLR. In the past, I would lug my pro DSLR camera on vacations and trips. This would be overwhelming and took away from the trip…I would have nice photos however… A few years ago I purchased a small Coolpix camera for trips and vacations. This way I can keep the camera in my pocket and enjoy the trip when not taking photographs.

Some DSLR functionality features to consider are: ISO Range, LCD size, Type of media it takes (SD, CF, etc.) Buffer Size, RAW mode, Bracketing, Shutter response and Focusing response speeds. These are specifications that you should carefully review before you decide on the best DSLR for you. If you are photographing weddings, a camera with fast focusing response and buffer speed is a must! It is also a good idea to test drive the camera in the store before making your investment. I also suggest looking up product reviews online and get recommendations from a pro photographer that you may know.

Photography Terms and Lingo:

Aperture:
The aperture is the opening formed by the blades of the iris or diaphragm in the lens, through which light passes to expose the film. Aperture size is usually given in f-numbers, the larger the number, the smaller the opening. Aperture size together with shutter speed determines the amount of light falling on the film (exposure). The aperture is sometimes called the "stop".

Camera Buffer:
After the sensor is exposed; the image data will be processed in the camera and then written to the storage card. A buffer inside a digital camera consists of RAM (random access memory) memory which temporarily holds the image information before it is written out to storage card. This speeds up the "time between shots" and allows burst (continuous) shooting mode.

Bracketing:
Best explained as the photographer taking numerous photos of the same thing using a variety of different camera settings. Bracketing is great when you are struggling to get a shot with exposure you like and that suits the image generally and helps ensure correct exposure of a photo when lighting in a scene is difficult.

DSLR:
(**D**igital **S**ingle **L**ens **R**eflex) A digital still image camera that uses a single lens reflex (SLR) mechanism. Most professional cameras have always been single lens reflex cameras, although analog. Digital SLRs began to emerge in the early 1990s, but became very popular after the turn of the century.

Film Speed/ISO/ASA:
ISO stands for International Standards Organization and numbers such as ISO 100 or ISO 400 etc. Film was always manufactured to be at a certain ASA. Digital cameras give you the ability adjust your sensitivity to light or ISO. The higher the number, the more sensitive or faster the film. Basically, the slower the film (low ISO No.) the sharper and clearer the photograph. Grainy effects can be achieved with fast films (high ISO No.).

Raw Mode:

Camera RAW files are also unprocessed, meaning all the photo processing is done on the computer. It is like taking a film negative to a dark room to be developed. The RAW file is the negative and the computer serves as the dark room.

Shutter Speed:

The shutter speed is the length of time that the light capture medium is open to the light. 1/30 is 1/30 of a second. Try to keep your shutter speed 1/90 - 1/125 or faster to avoid camera blur. Anything less than 1/60 and you will need to either use a tripod or be very aware of your camera movement. It all depends upon you. For some, 1/60 may be too slow a shutter speed while others can work at 1/25th. Also note that the longer the focal length, telephoto vs wide angle lens, the more camera movement will affect image sharpness.

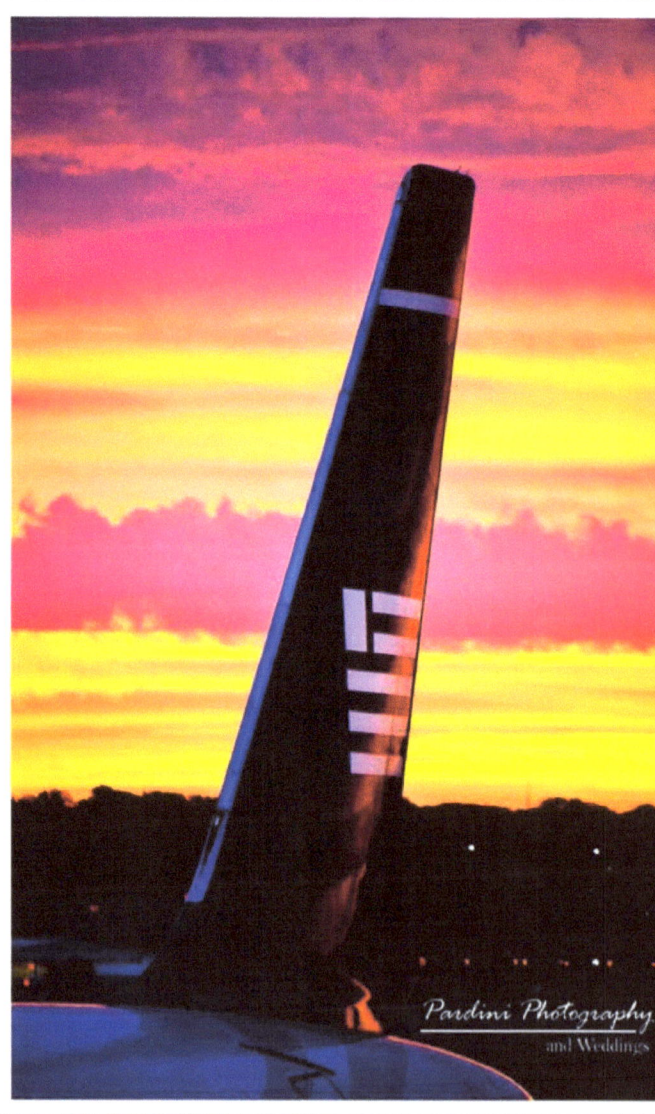

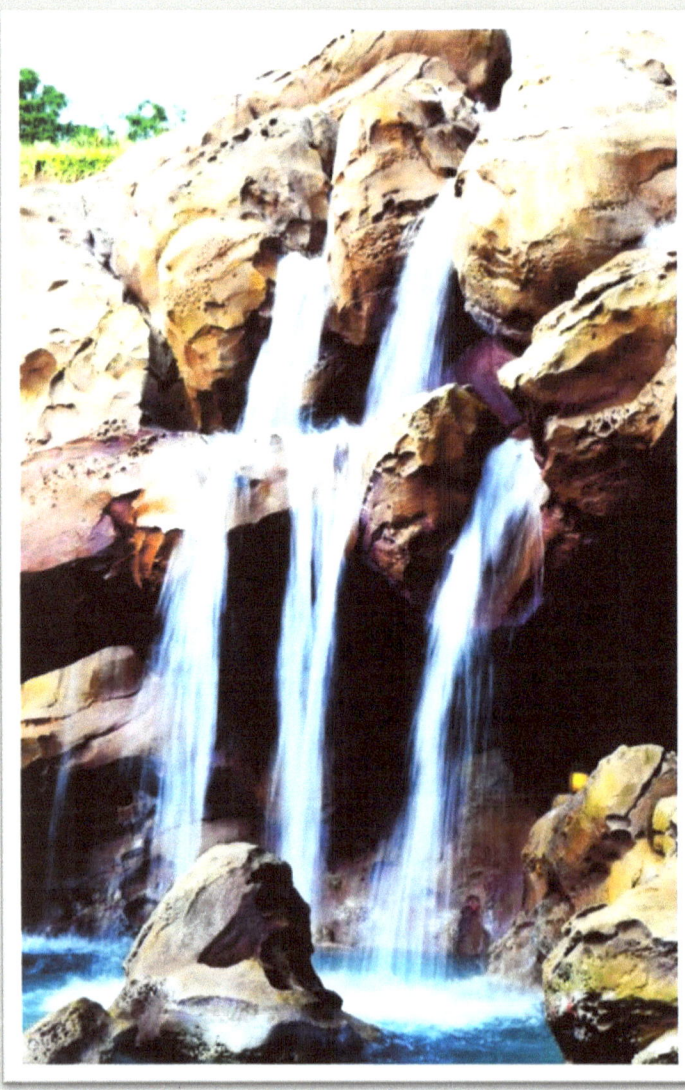

Why is Wedding Photography So Expensive?

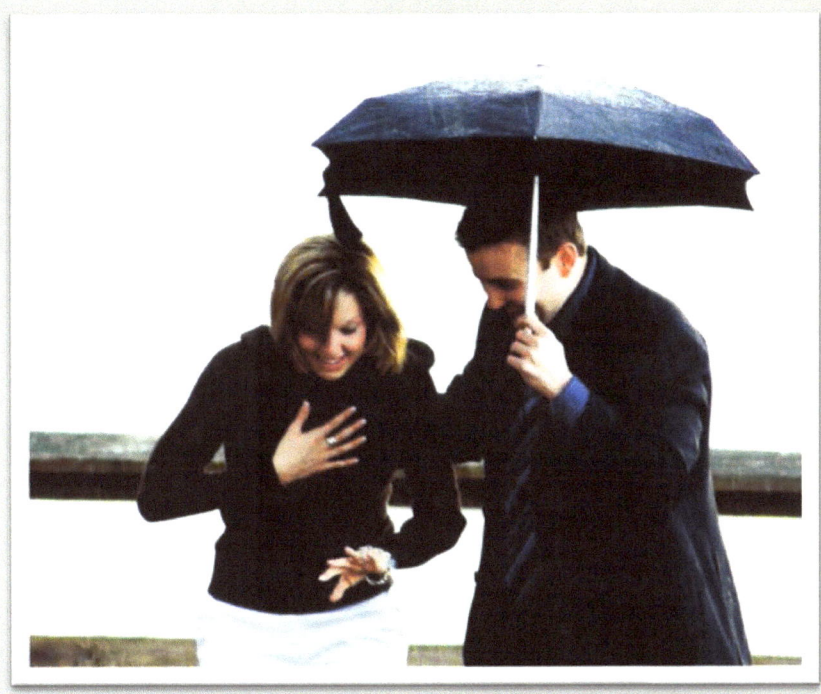

We are often asked why photography is so expensive, especially wedding photography…

Well, wedding photography is not cheap– but have you ever thought about why that might be??? Well, hopefully this will shine some light on this subject!

Spring is in full bloom, so the hectic wedding season is about to arrive… Lately we have been getting a lot of couples asking why wedding photography prices are so expensive and if you can lower the cost of your packages… While it may seem like wedding photographers live an amazing life by charging through the roof for a day of work, it's hardly the case...

It goes without saying that weddings are a costly event. From the venue to the caterer to the wedding favors…the budget just keeps getting higher. It often seems that wedding photographers are charging a large chunk of that budget. But not too many people understand why wedding photography prices are so high! It's because of the associated costs of being a wedding photographer and what goes into it.

Being a good photographer is an expensive investment. Sure, you can find cheap wedding photographers out there, but they're cheap because they've possible cut corners on equipment and in other areas too! Please excuse my wording on this: or they're just plain stupid (you hired cheap and stupid?) So let's take a look at what goes into a photographer's overhead that adds up to the final cost of your wedding photographer:

- Labor Costs: This one is pretty standard across all industries. A photographer's work doesn't end when your wedding does. After the 8 + hours they've put in working (on a Saturday, no less) at your nuptials, the photographer spends hours and hours editing your images so you get a wide array of perfect photographs by which to remember your day. It's not uncommon to work another 20-30 hours editing the photographs and post production work after the wedding.

- Equipment: The equipment a photographer uses is not your typical point-and-shoot camera. High-end cameras can cost $5,000 - $10,000 per camera! Photographers also carry back-up equipment in case their primary equipment fails, which adds to the cost of the wedding photography prices. Some photographers use a deprecation percentage added to their overall pricing. Prices of computers and editing programs like Photoshop costs begin to skyrocket too. Photoshop alone is $800+.

- Website and search engines: In this day and age, a photographer has to market with a very high-tech, professional website, which can cost a lot to design and maintain if the photographer does not have web design skills. It's not unreasonable to spend over $5000 a year on website updates, and online marketing such as the sponsored links on Google. We do our website in-house, however, the cost for webhosting and search engine optimizations can rack up!

- Advertising: In that same vein, photographers also have to spend money on other types of advertising such as ads in the newspaper, business cards and brochures.

- Photo Extras: If you knew how much albums cost you'd have a heart attack. Albums are extraordinarily expensive and are often added into the wedding photography prices. Don't forget the time it takes to design them as well.

- Education: The higher the degree a photographer has or continuing education under his/her belt, the better techniques and specializations will be used while shooting a wedding. As everything else, that education comes at a cost through instructors, college degrees, extra classes and seminars, etc.

So while you may be asking, 'why does photographer X cost so much more than photographer Y?' the answer might be simple: Photographer X has spent more money developing his or her business into a distinguished photography service, which ends up costing more money than an inexperienced photographer that may not perform to the level of service that will meet your expectations! Remember - Photography is a way of feeling, of touching, of loving. What you have caught on film is captured forever... it remembers little things, long after you have forgotten everything...

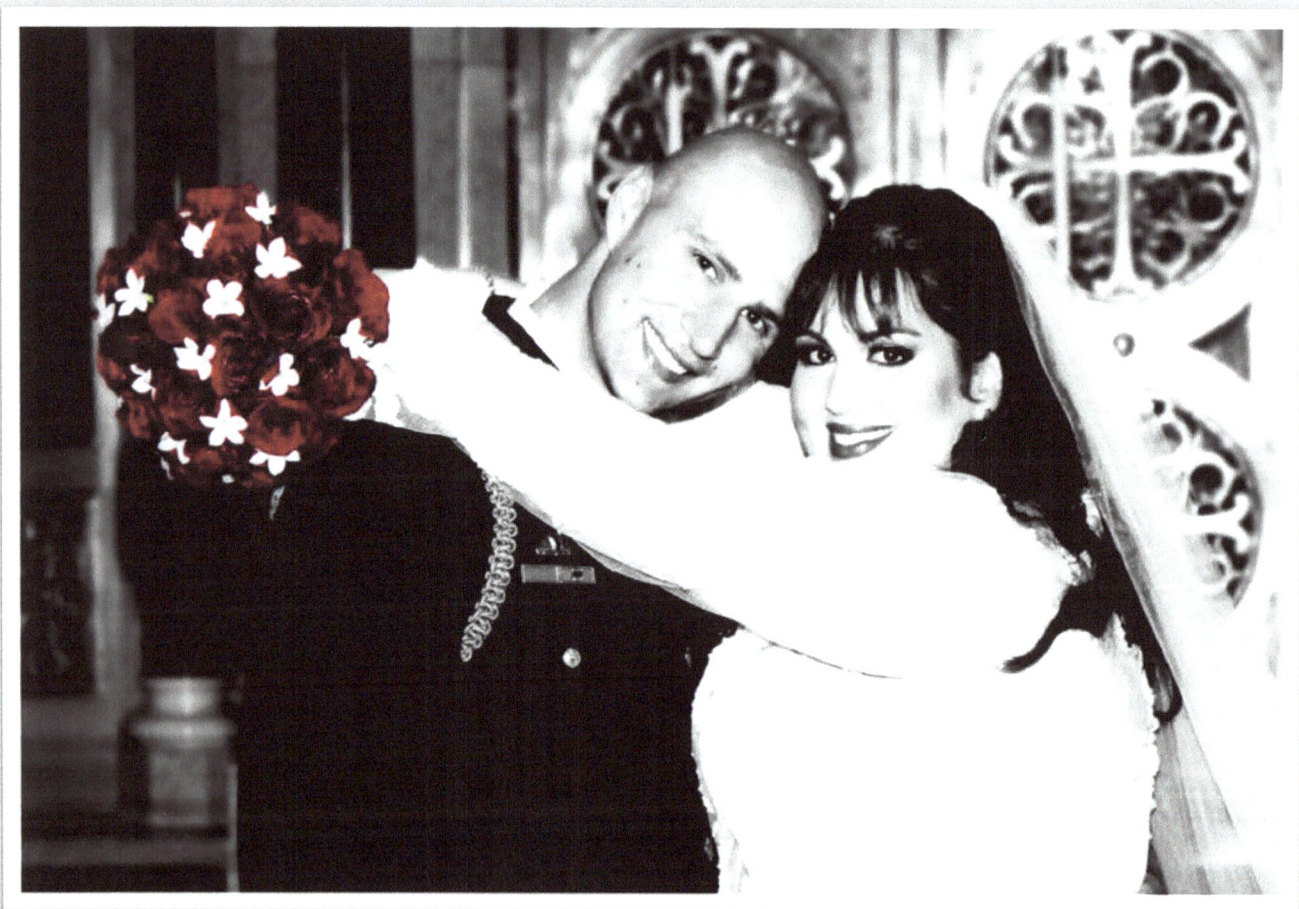

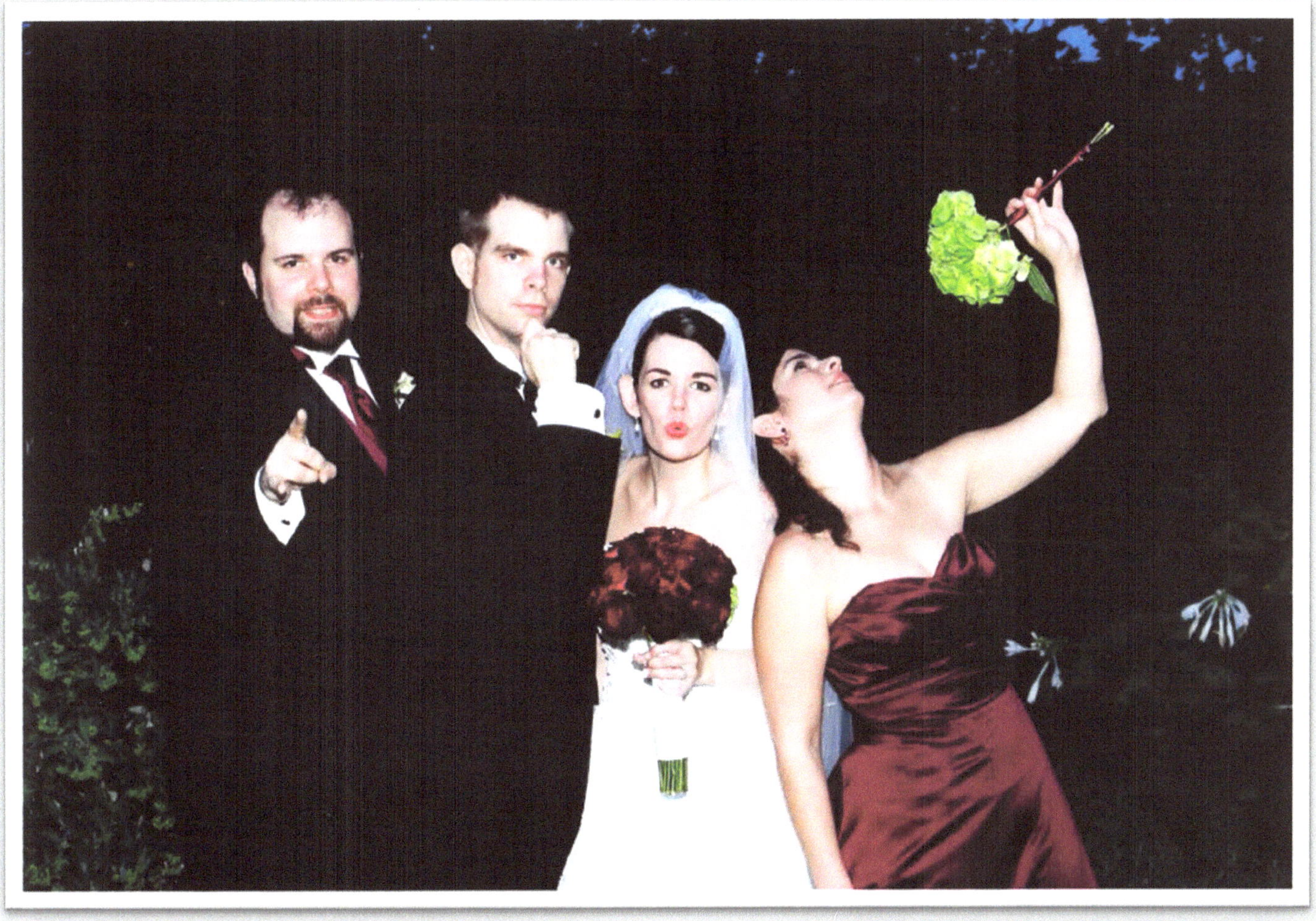

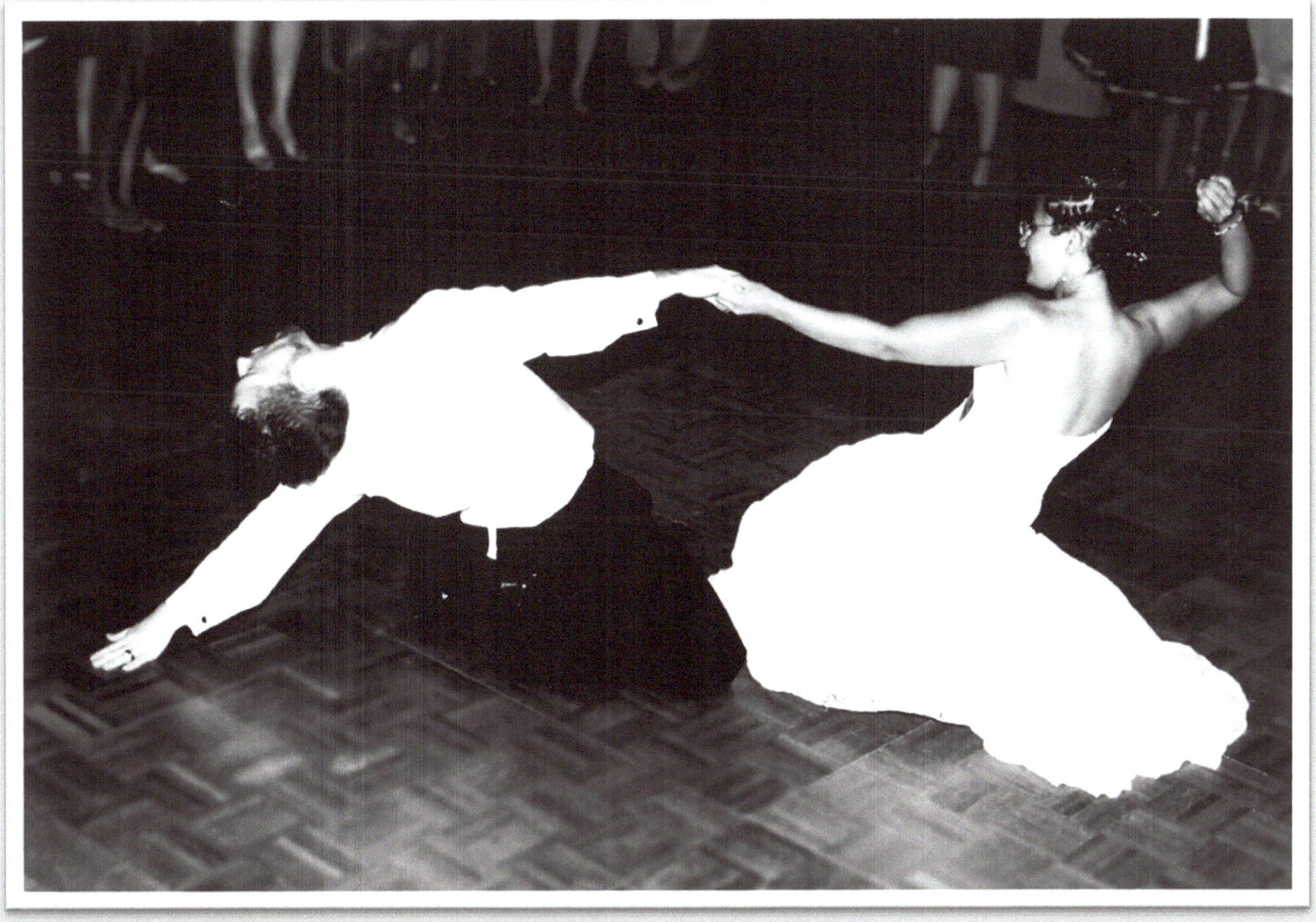

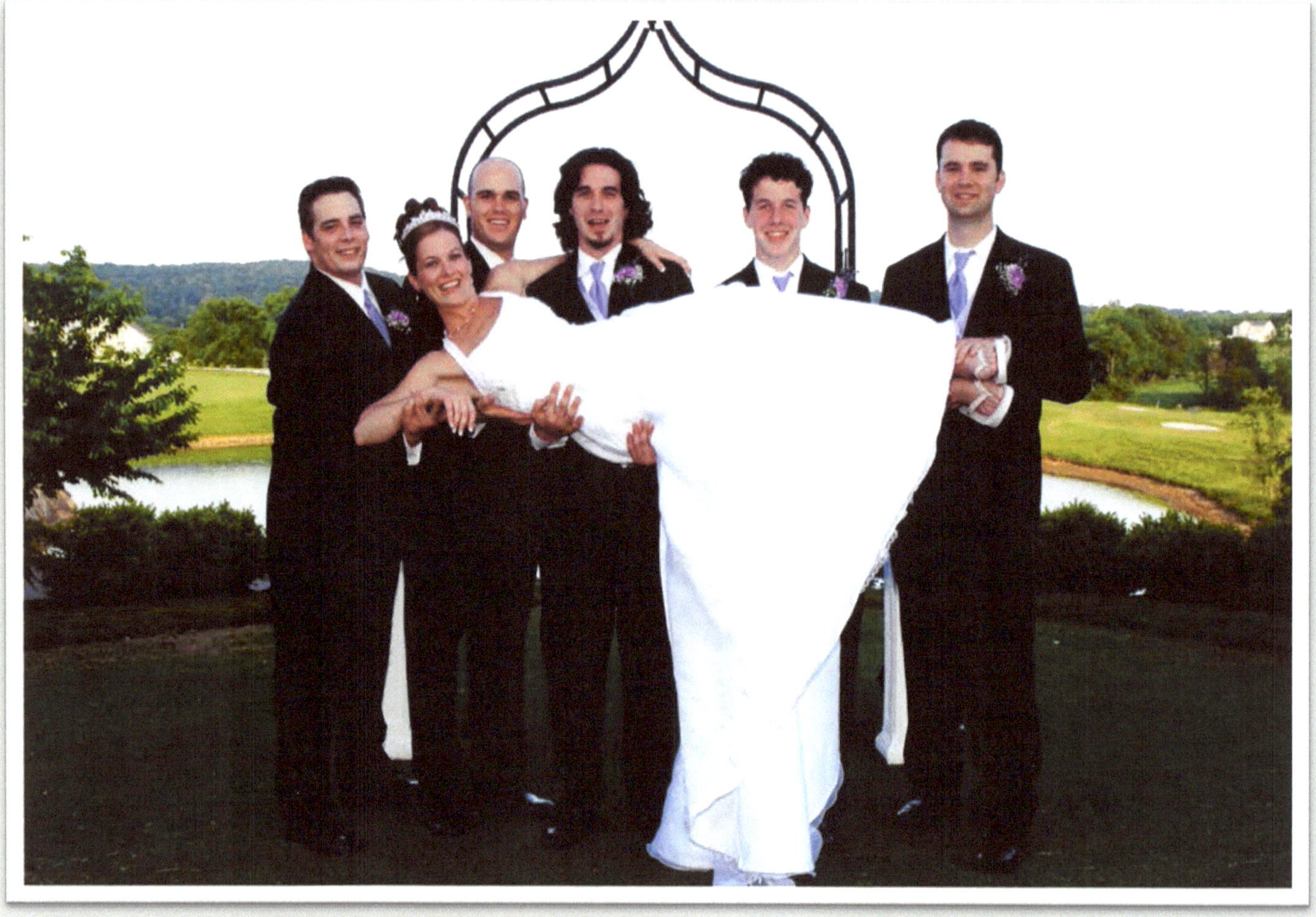

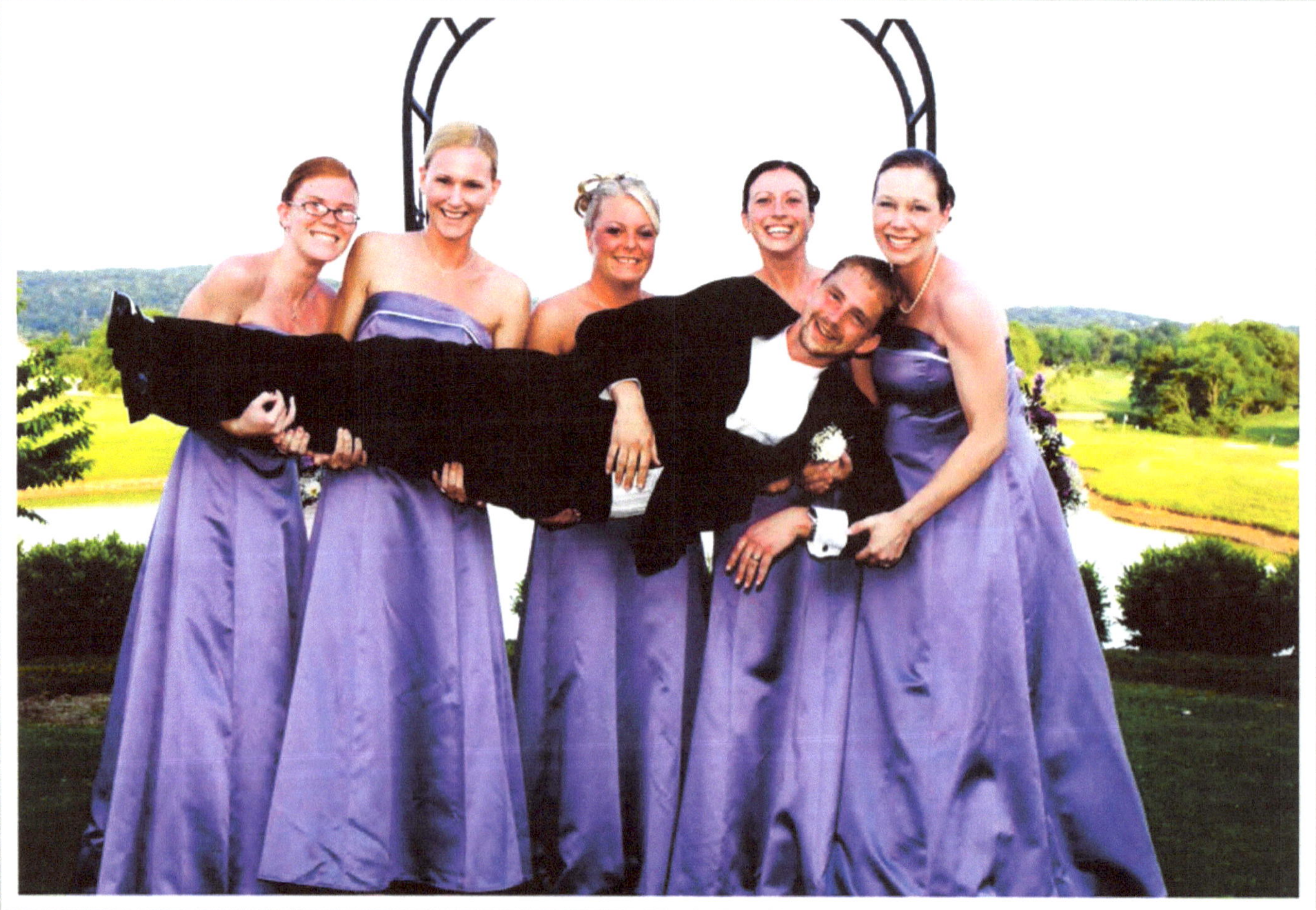

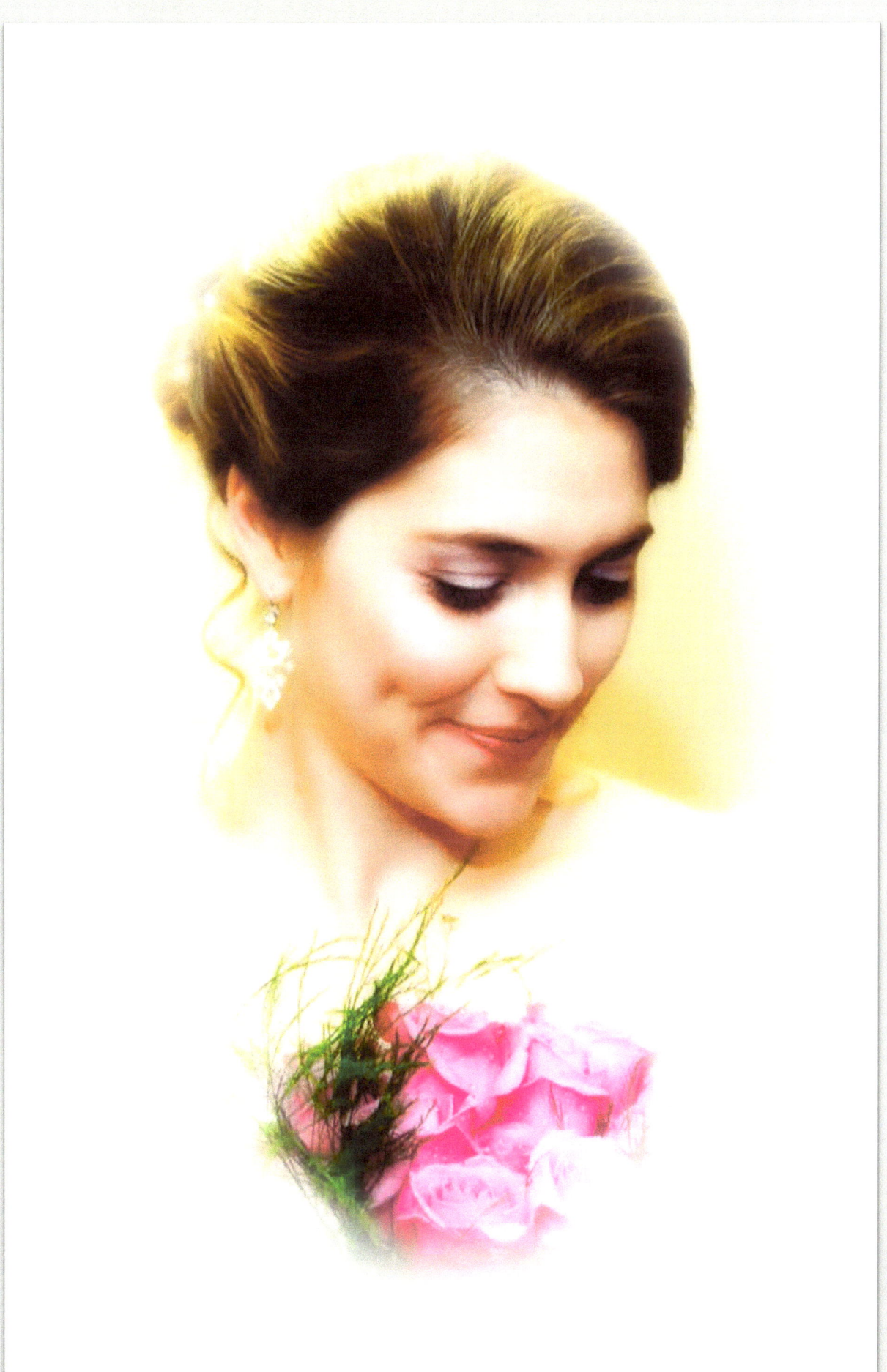

Understanding Your Camera's Histogram

You might have heard the term 'histogram' and wondered what that was…The histogram is a graphic representation of the tonal range in a photograph, and its analysis of the image's tonal range provides a precise check on exposure. The histogram depicts the range of tones in an image from the darkest on the left of the graph (0 in digital terms) to the lightest on the right side (255 in digital terms).

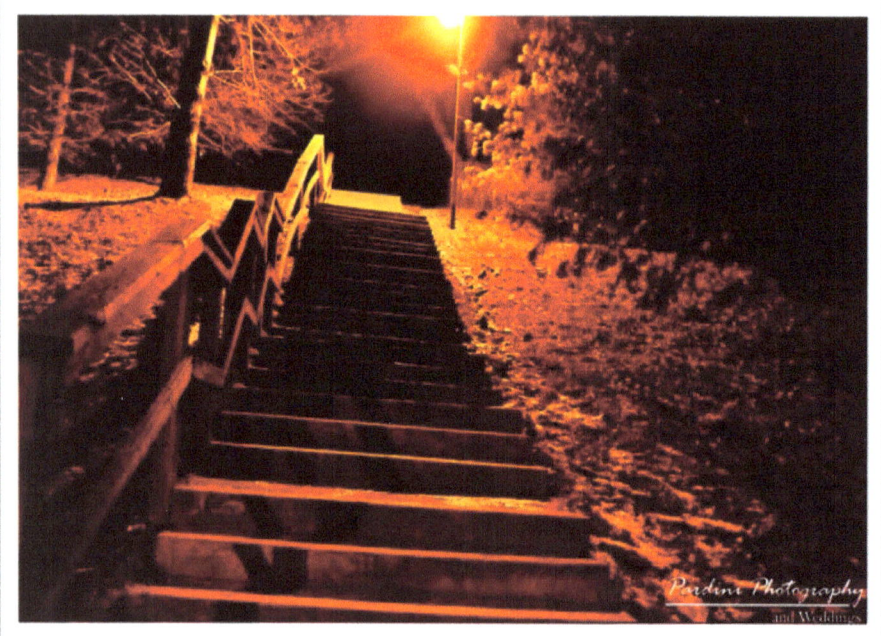

You might think of it this way: a light meter reads the scene before you take the photo; the histogram analyzes the photo you've just taken. You can choose to have the histogram appear on the camera's LCD along with the playback display of your photo (see your D-SLR manual for the exact procedure).

That's what the histogram is. But why is it an important, fundamental tool of digital photography? Simply because your understanding of the histogram will tell you if it's necessary to adjust your exposure, and it will indicate how to make that adjustment.

The first thing to realize, though, is that it's not always necessary to use the histogram. In fact, selective use is best. Few if any photographers look at the histogram for each and every photo they take. In the majority of instances, your camera's meter will accurately and precisely set the correct exposure for the scene.

But you should check the histogram when a scene's lighting is especially tricky; when there are areas of deep shadow and bright light in the same scene; and when you're going to take a series of images in the same setting and want to be sure your exposure is right on target.

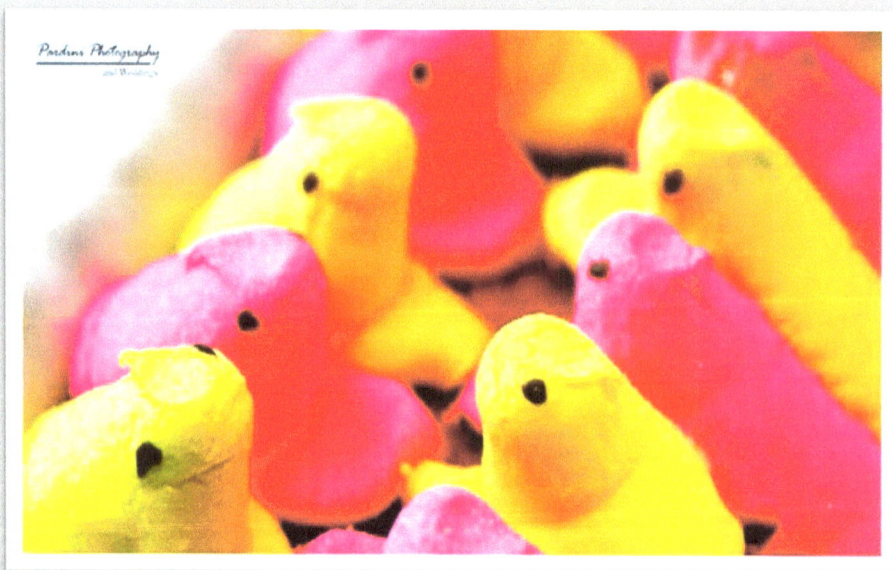

A glance at the histogram will tell you if parts of your photo are over- or underexposed. Overexposure means lack of detail in the highlights; underexposure, loss of detail in the shadows. The histogram will instantly reveal the situation: a heavy concentration at the left side of the graph means the image is underexposed and you've lost detail in the shadow areas; a heavy concentration at the right means your highlights may be blown out. The remedy? You can increase your shutter speed, close down aperture or lower your ISO to correct overexposure; the opposite settings will serve to correct an underexposure.

Here's something you might want to use in connection with the histogram: the highlight overexposure warning. Set this option (again, see your manual for the specific activation method) and areas of overexposure will blink in the playback image. When you see these flashes of light—most people call them "blinkies"—you'll know exactly which areas of the image are overexposed.

Several higher end D-SLRs feature secondary, color histograms. Choose to display them and you'll see three small graphs that show the intensity of the RGB (red, green and blue) color values in the scene. If you need to adjust these values, the camera's white balance control is the way to do it.

Some D-SLRs also allow you to magnify specific areas of the photo on playback so you can check exposure and detail rendering in very specific parts of the image. In effect, you're directing the histogram's area of analysis.

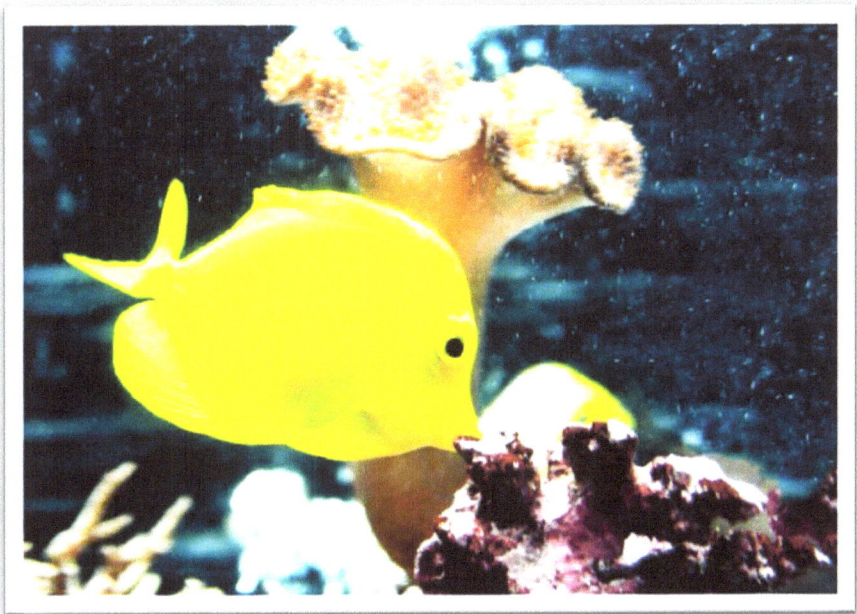

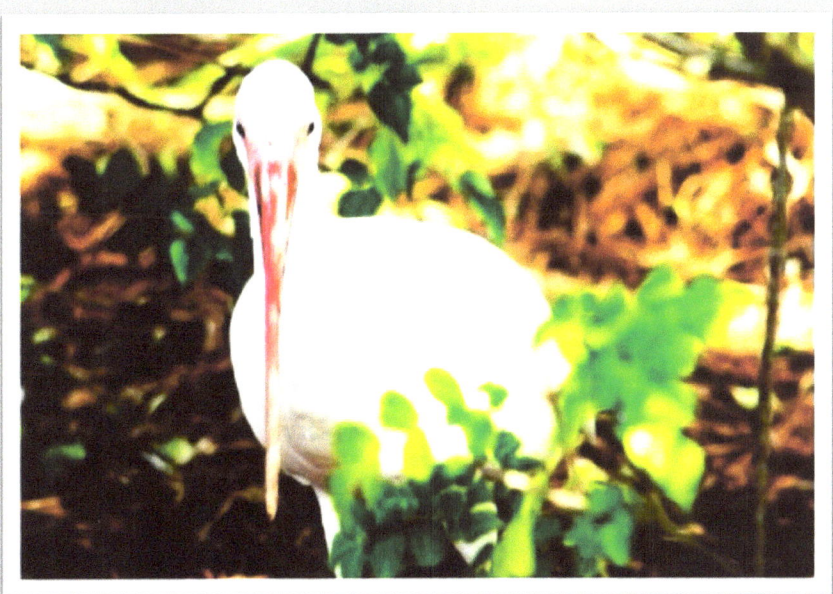

Understanding Photography Lingo

In any field of arts or sciences, there's a lot of jargon that's flung around, and seeing as photography is both, it means even more jargon. So you shouldn't feel put off if you don't know all the technical terms other photographers use. Some of these terms you probably already know, but to fill you in on a few that you may not know, here's a list of some of the most common words you'll come across.

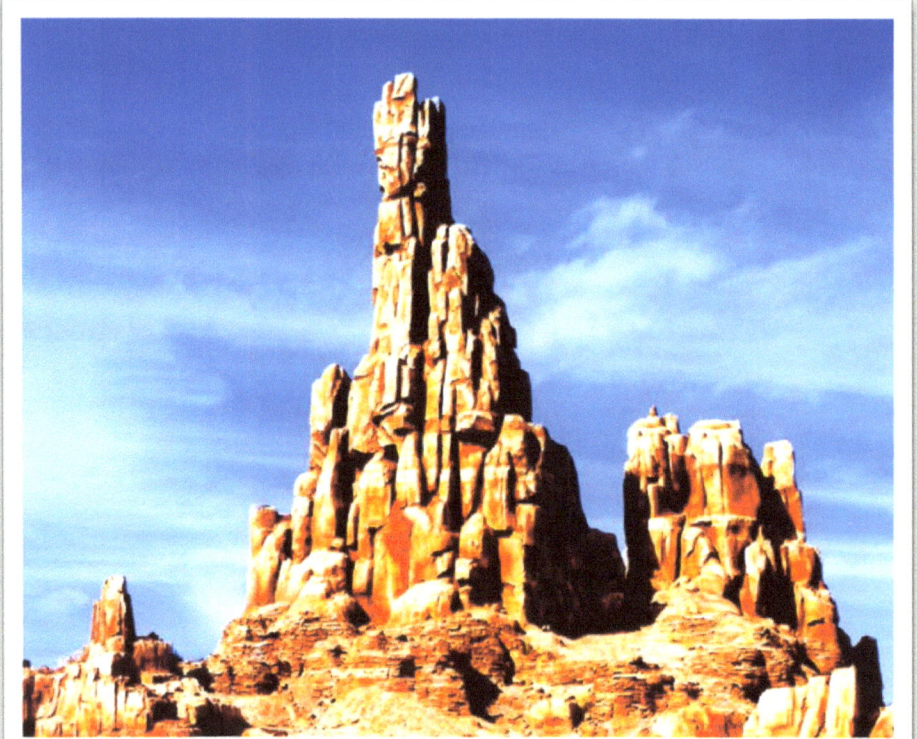

Stop Down: Refers to changing the aperture by increasing the f-number so that the aperture opening becomes smaller. It is often recommended to stop down when you need a larger depth-of-field or if you're shooting wide open and want your photo to be sharper. Most lenses are sharpest when stopped down a few times from their maximum aperture.

Full-Frame, Crop-Frame: The sensor of a full-frame digital camera is the same size as what is captured with a 35mm film camera. A crop-frame camera is anything smaller than a full-frame. The most common cropped cameras are 1.5 or 1.6 times smaller than a full-frame.

Backlight: Strong light source coming from behind your subject. Backlighting is often tricky to deal with compared to other lighting conditions; however, it is also commonly used in adjacent with other lights in commercial photography.

Candid: An unopposed photograph. A candid photo is one where the subject is acting naturally and does not seem to be aware of the photographer.

Hard Light, Soft Light: Strong, direct light is referred to as hard light whereas diffused light is called soft light. For instance, the sun on a clear day would be a hard light. On a cloudy day, it would be a soft light.

Exposure Compensation: A control on some cameras that lets you under- or overexpose the "correct" exposure settings set automatically by the camera. Can be very handy for when a camera generally properly exposes a scene but is consistently off by a small amount.

Fill Flash: Flash used to fill in the shadows on a subject. These shadows may be natural or caused by another flash. A fill flash does not always eliminate shadows, but fills them in to reduce contrast.

Noise: A random array of off-color pixels that can vary in brightness also. Noise is generally created by using high ISO settings and is worse with small sensor cameras. It is an unwanted effect that can be improved with in-camera noise reduction or software, but often makes the image softer.

Chromatic Aberration: A type of distortion that arises when the colors of an image do not align properly. Some poor-quality lenses show chromatic aberration on the edges of the frame resulting in a fringe of colors that appears blurry. There are other forms of aberration, but this is the most common.

Ambient Light: Any light that is not artificial. The term ambient light is often used in conjunction with artificial lighting since it is important to balance out the natural and unnatural light in a scene.

Image Artifact: Noticeable flaws in a photograph that arise from image degradation. This commonly happens when the image in saved multiple times in a compressed image format such as a jpeg.

Bulb: A setting on cameras that lets you open the shutter for as long as the shutter button is held. Used for long exposures, often at night.

Back-Focusing, Front-Focusing: A tendency of a lens to consistently focus slightly in front of or behind a subject when properly focused. This is an unwanted flaw that may be able to be fixed with the camera's settings or may need to be fixed by the manufacturer.

Bokeh: Out of focus points of light. Most easily seen when a camera is shot with a wide aperture and shallow depth-of-field. The shape of the bokeh is determined by the shape of the aperture.

Bounce Flash: Any artificial light that is reflected off of a surface and back onto the subject. Bounce flash can provide a much softer and more wide-spread light than the original source.

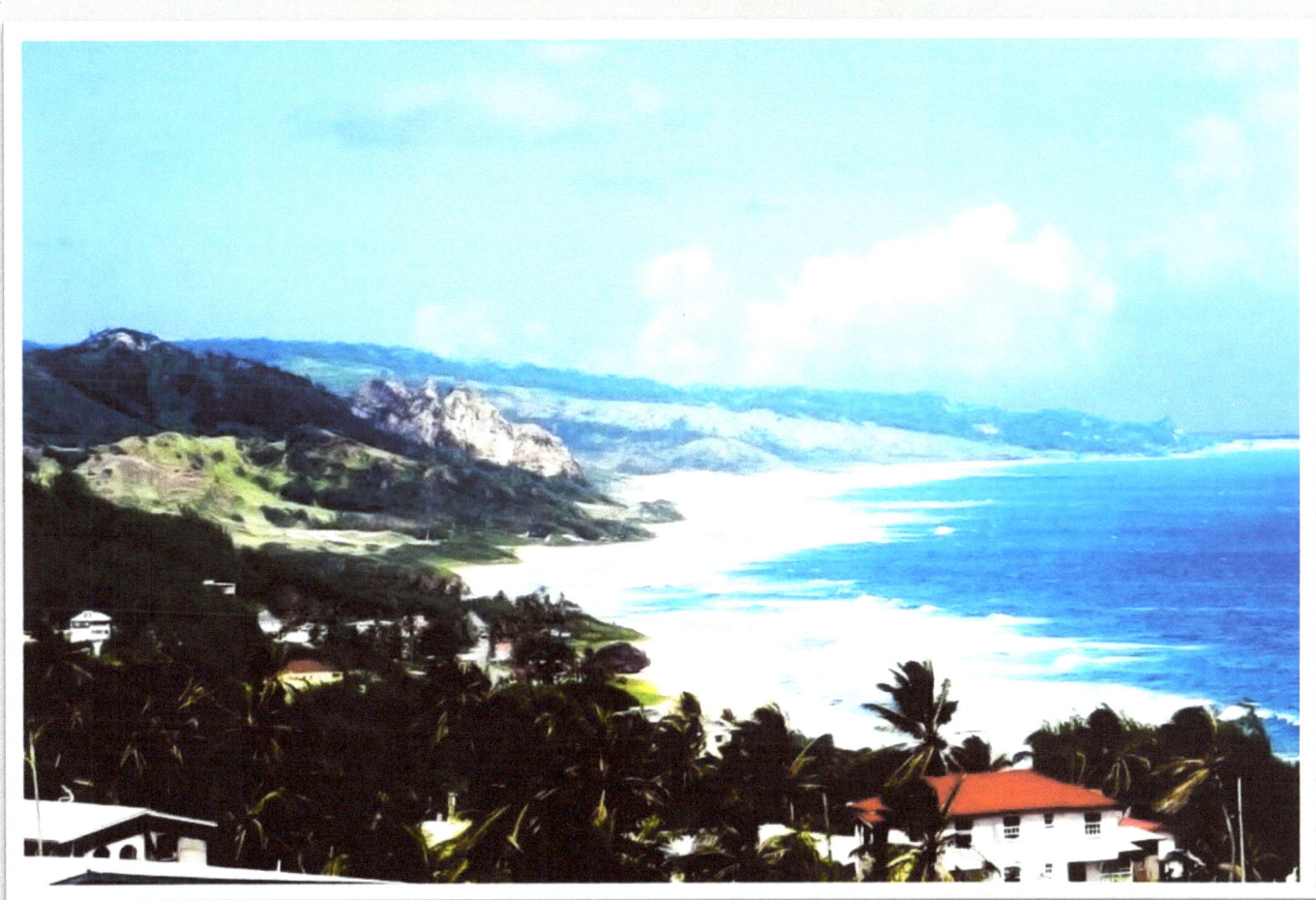

About the Author

Craig Pardini was born in Bethesda, Maryland, Saturday, February 8, 1975 at 7:26AM. Craig started to become interested in photography sometime back around the age of 8. Ever since, Craig would try to capture anything of interest. In 1990, Craig first started his formal studies as a photographer and was offered a teacher's assistant position for that very same photography course the following year. Throughout school, Craig took the interest of sports photography and became the school's main sports photographer. In 1993, Craig was offered a full scholarship to Brooks Institute to further his photography, communication arts, and graphic arts studies.

Craig holds the prestigious Masters of Fine Arts in Photography degree (M.P.R.) and is a certified master professional

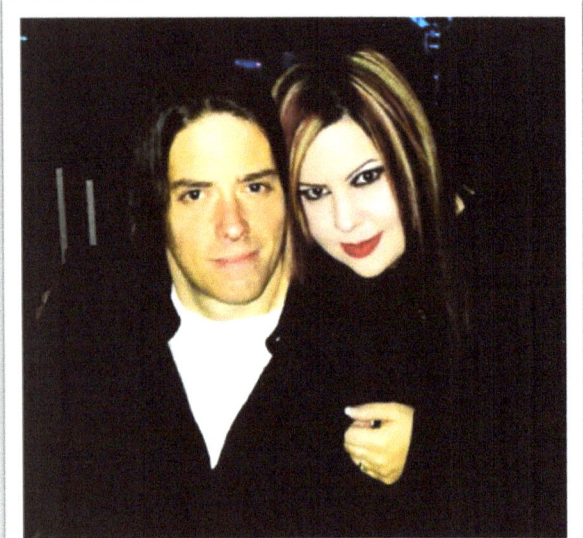

wedding and portrait photographer. Craig is an active member in numerous photography organizations such as: Professional Photographers of America, American Image Press, International Freelance Photographers Organization and The National Association of Photoshop Professionals.

In 1994, Craig established Pardini Images and started photographing weddings professionally. Craig's first wedding was a referral from his photography professor in 1994. Between 1994 and 1999, Craig photographed many different weddings and formal events independently.

In 1999, Craig married his soul mate Kathy Ireland and shortly thereafter, Pardini Images changed to Pardini Photography and Weddings. Since Y2K, the team of Craig and Kathy made many differences in people's lives by documenting special, once in a lifetime moments with excellence!

Craig and Kathy are always continuing their knowledge on the latest cutting edge photography technology. Craig frequently attends photography seminars and Photography / Photoshop continuing educational courses. In late 2008, Craig started instructing a photography class / program for individuals with autism. In 2009, Craig was inducted into the IFPO Photographers Hall of Fame. In 2010, Craig started small instructional photography seminars on how to take better photographs and Photoshop editing.

Most of the time you will see Craig with a camera in hand or pulling out his Android phone to take snapshots. During trips and outings, Craig prefers to use a Nikon point and shoot or his camera phone for fun photos. Only during professional events will Craig pull out his pro cameras.

Kathy has the eye for detail and the knowledge of transforming a great photograph into an exceptional work of art. Kathy uses Photoshop to edit every photo to a 'T' to make photographs to look the absolute best that they can be! In the photos that she edits, you will never see an air vent, light switch, ugly exit sign, or any other blemish, etc. Kathy takes the time to remove all obtrusive objects so the viewer will focus on the subject and not the blemish...

In conclusion, all photographs that Craig and Kathy capture, will take your breath away. You will brush back tears by reliving the memories through these photographs that will be passed around the family room for generations to come.